ISLAND ADVENTURES

An Outdoors Guide to Vancouver Island

Richard K. Blier

Orca Book Publishers

Canadian Cataloguing in Publication Data

Blier, Richard, 1952-
    Island adventures

    Includes index.
    ISBN 0-920501-28-1

    1. Vancouver Island (B.C.) — Description and travel
— Guide-books.   I. Title.
FC3844.2.B63 1989   917.11'34044   C89-091261-0
F1089.V3B63 1989

Orca Book Publishers
P.O. Box 5626, Stn. B
Victoria, B.C. V8R 6S4
Canada

Maps by Ronald T. Blier.
Cover design by Susan Fergusson.
Printed and bound in Canada by Hignell Printing Ltd.

This book is dedicated to my mother and father, who instilled in me at an early age a love and appreciation for the outdoors; to all the people who have accompanied me on my Island Adventures *over the years; and to all fellow backwoods browsers.*

Acknowledgements

The author wishes to thank the following persons whose help made *Island Adventures* a reality. For assistance with mileages: R.T. Blier, Jon Chant, Martin Nicholas, Tim Oldford, Frank Bannard, Graeme McFayden, Marion Wightman, Bill Hadden, Reg Geary, and Jack Langejan. Thanks to employees at regional tourist bureaus, B.C. government offices and logging companies for their time and valuable information. Thanks to R.T. Blier for his maps; Bill Hadden for his photos; Marion Wightman for secretarial duties; and Reg Geary for keeping my vehicles logging-road ready all these years. Word-processing assistance: Brenda Gerth, R.T. Blier, Angelie VanderByl. Special thanks to Bob Tyrrell and Orca Book Publishers for initiating and supporting this project.

Contents

Lower Island

Central Island

North Island

About this book

Island Adventures is divided into three distinct regions: **Lower Island**; **Central Vancouver Island** and **North Island**.

Thirty-five Island outings are described. Destinations range from well-known provincial parks, B.C. Forest Service locations and primitive wilderness campsites to hiking trails, fishing lakes, canoeing districts and four-wheeling regions. These are reached by main highways, secondary backroads and logging mainlines. Some areas require a canoe, kayak or boat for water access. Trips are broken down into six sections:

1. In Brief:

Each trip is introduced with mention of what to expect and key points of interest are noted.

2. Access:

For quick reference, this section lists major access routes to each locale and gives information on the type of roads and general road conditions that may be encountered (gravel, logging mainline, rough secondary spur etc.). Any entry restrictions are also noted.

3. Description:

This section gives a detailed look at each trip including distances in kilometres and miles, background information, and suggested areas for further exploration. I have not included every milestone along the way; part of the fun and excitement of any jaunt is coming upon the unexpected — whether it be a scenic vista, an intriguing side road or secluded campsite. Major points of interest, important intersections and access roads are noted, however. You may find a slight variance in the milestones given. No two vehicles are exactly alike and no two people drive in an identical manner. Slippery or frosty roads can also alter mileages somewhat.

4. Contacts:

Here you will find hints for pre-trip planning: who to contact for regional access restrictions and road conditions, updates on hauling and active logging areas, and other pertinent information. Listings may include district logging company offices, B.C. Forest Service regional offices or Parks Branch sources. Visitors should also check with local Chambers of Commerce, tourist bureaus and Infocentres for additional information. Every effort has been made to include current phone numbers and addresses. Occasionally, though, some may change without warning. (In the last few years, even some logging company names have been changed.)

5. Maps/Guides:

Most logging companies publish recreational guides to their logging divisions. There are some B.C. Forest Service pamphlets also available.

Topographical maps are indispensable on any outing, particularly on the backroads. Any relevant maps or guides available will appear under this heading. (Addresses where you may obtain these items are listed at the back of the book.) When used in conjunction with *Island Adventures*, you're sure to discover some island destination you may not have been aware of before.

On many trips highlighted in *Island Adventures*, you may require only one small-scale map and one or two of the larger-scale maps listed in this section. This will depend on what you plan to do and where you decide to go. If you're the type of person who can spend hours studying maps and charts, you may want to purchase all the topographical sheets for your chosen route. Not all maps are up to date. In many cases, using a topographical map alongside logging-company road guides is practical.

6.Nearest Services:

This section tells you where to find the closest gas, groceries and other services.

Logging Road Travel on Vancouver Island

Vancouver Island is criss-crossed by networks of logging roads. These fall under three general classifications:

1. Restricted-Access Roads:

Roads falling under this classification run through active logging areas and include mainlines on which hauling is taking place. Public entry on these roads is limited to after working hours on weekdays and on weekends and holidays. In some regions, these routes are closed to the public at all times, for safety and security reasons. It's a good idea to call area logging offices to check on access limitations prior to venturing on these roads. Restricted roads are identified by a red, octagonal stop sign.

2. Combined-use Roads:

Roads in this category are open to the public 24-hours-a-day; however, they are also used by industrial traffic which can include loaded and unloaded logging trucks, heavy equipment or logging company buses and pickups. Travellers MUST yield the right-of-way to ALL logging company vehicles by pulling well over to the shoulder of the road and STOPPING. A yellow, inverted triangle indentifies these roads.

3. Inactive Roads:

These roads are open to the public at all hours. Industrial traffic is rare as these arteries generally go into inactive logging districts. They may be rough or entirely impassable due to lack of maintenance and washouts. They are indentified by a welcoming green circle.

Some roads are signposted as Private Industrial Roads. Read and obey all posted notices on any road you travel. Remember to use your headlights at all times on the logging roads!

Any logging road may be closed due to high forest-fire hazard. Closures due to active logging or unsafe conditions — such as washouts and deteriorating bridges — may also restrict access. Off-season adventurers should keep in mind that the backroads are highly susceptible to the whims of mother nature. Heavy rains can quickly wash away roadbeds or turn a passable route into a washboard of potholes and deep puddles. Heavy snows may block some higher elevations entirely over the winter. Make sure your vehicle is in good repair. Check your spare tire (some people carry two) and bring along extra water and oil. Don't forget to gas up if you're journeying into remote regions. Remember to tell someone where you're going and when you'll be back.

In some areas it may seem as if you are the first one to discover some pristine nook in the forest. Don't bet on it. Chances are good that someone has been there before. But by practising low-impact camping and leaving the site in a natural state, you can help ensure that future visitors who might come upon your "secret spot" will have that sense of a wilderness experience which nowadays is becoming more and more elusive.

Many wilderness campsites are user-maintained — each visitor is required to clean up prior to his or her departure. There will always be a minority of careless campers who litter forest campsites and fire pits with refuse. We can all do our part by leaving our sites tidy for the next visitors. But enough of the preliminaries; let's head off for some Island adventuring.

Trip I: Victoria to Port Renfrew

In Brief:

The 100-kilometre (62-mile) drive from Victoria to Port Renfrew winds along the south coast of Vancouver Island with much to offer the outdoorsman. Whether you enjoy hiking, salt- or fresh-water fishing, backroading, camping or great West Coast scenery, this is the jaunt for you.

Access:

Take Highway 1 to the Colwood overpass and follow the Sooke cutoff onto Highway 14. The route is mostly paved highway with winding sections. The 8 km (5 mi) of gravel has been improved with an oil base and pea gravel. Watch for narrow bridges and some sharp corners. Industrial traffic is frequent on this combined-use road.

Description:

The first part of this jaunt runs from Colwood, just outside Victoria, through the Sooke Hills to the community of Sooke. Follow Highway 1 to the Colwood overpass and take the Sooke cutoff onto Highway 14. Happy Valley Road provides access to the marinas catering to salt-water fishermen who frequent Sooke waters and the Beecher and Pedder Bay areas.

Gillespie Road, just beyond the Seventeen Mile House, is the main road going in to the East Sooke Park trails. This wilderness Capital Regional District (CRD) park features a variety of trails leading in to mountain vistas and seaside cliffs. Old mine sites, petroglyphs and the view across Juan de Fuca Strait add to the park's charm.

At Saseenos, Harbourview Road intersects Highway 14, just over 4 km (2.5 mi) from the Gillespie Road turn. This rugged route is the one to take for Sooke Mountain Provincial Park, Shields, Grassie and Crabapple lakes.

8

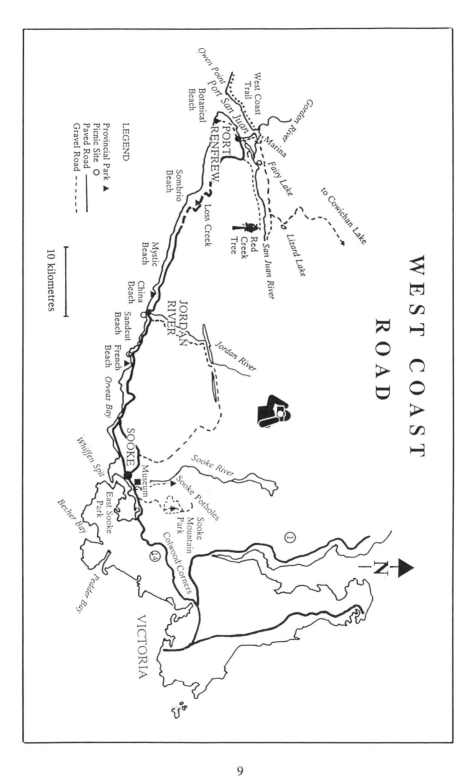

WEST COAST ROAD

LEGEND

Provincial Park ▲
Picnic Site ○
Paved Road ——
Gravel Road -----

10 kilometres

9

French Beach is just one of many west coast strands accessible from the West Coast Road.

It is susceptible to washouts and may require a four-by-four to negotiate the rougher sections.

Even if you don't drive in you can always hike. Mount Manuel Quimper is one option for climbers and north of Crabapple Lake is Empress Mountain and a fire lookout. There are many side roads in this region, so be sure to carry maps with you. Sooke River Road is just before the bridge over the Sooke River.ⁱ Take this road to Sooke Potholes Provincial Park for swimming, riverside trails and the potholes carved into the riverbed by this river.

We'll mark the Sooke River bridge km/mi 0 for this trip. It's about 26 km (16 mi) to this point from the Sooke cutoff on Highway 1. Phillips Road, directly across the bridge, is where the Sooke Region Museum is located. The staff have a wealth of local history to share with visitors and the museum is worth a stop. Tourist information for Sooke and Jordan River is also available here.

The road goes through Sooke west to Gordon Beach, a wide, rocky shoreline on Orveas Bay. Here there is an expansive view of Juan de Fuca Strait. French Beach Provincial Park (km 23.2/mi 14.5) has 69 tent and R.V. campsites, woodland trails and a nice beachfront. Those preferring a serviced campground can base here for day-tripping. At km 25.7 (mi 16) a side road on the left leads to a Western Forest Products (WFP) picnic site. There is a small parking area here at the turnaround surrounded by thick bushes. You'll discover a number of wilderness beaches that can be reached by trails of varying lengths on the road to Port Renfrew. Sandcut Beach (km 30/mi 18.5) is accessed by a short path from the parking lot to the sea. From here, beachwalkers can negotiate the alternating sand and cobble shore eastward to Jordan River.

From Point No Point the mountains over in Washington state are impressive on a clear day. The road descends a steep hill down to the Jordan River townsite (km 33.6/mi 21). WFP has a campsite and picnic area on the point of land right before the Jordan River bridge. This site fills up with RV'ers over the summer. This limited-service location is a popular base camp for day trippers. China Beach Provincial Park is about 5 km (3 mi) west of Jordan River. The trail to the sea winds through the forest, down a sharp hill to emerge on the gravel beach. It's a wild place when the wind is up, tossing breakers onto the sloping shore. At low tides, some sandy sections are exposed. Weekend beachcombers frequent China Beach year round. No camping or open fires are permitted.

Mystic Beach (km 39.6/mi 24.5) is reached via a steep path that plunges through the rain forest down to the seashore. As with most of the beaches on the Port Renfrew run, it takes less time to head into the wilderness strands that it does coming out.

On your way to Port Renfrew you'll only encounter about 8 km (5 mi) of gravel. This section has been improved with pea gravel on an oil base; there are still some blind corners, steep hills and narrow bridges. These Bailey bridges are closer to Renfrew. The pavement ends at km 52.4 (mi 32.5).

Loss Creek Provincial Park (km 53.7/mi 33.3) is relatively unknown to many. It is marked by the large butt-log bridge over Loss Creek where the Renfrew Road curves to the left at a junction with an active logging road. This is an undeveloped park; however, you can walk along the creek by following primitive trails. A tiny waterfall is located on a rock wall on the north side of Loss Creek.

The road will climb a grade and soon pass the first of two access points for Sombrio Beach. At km 57.2 (mi 35.5) turn left onto an old logging road which deadends at the trailhead and a small parking area. The route down to the trailhead is steep and usually muddy. You might spot a black bear foraging in the logging slash in this area. If you're the type of person that likes a rugged trail, choose this one if you're going to Sombrio. The second approach to Sombrio Point is the logging road on the left at km 57.6 (mi 35.7). Turn at the signpost and follow the switchback to the parking area, a few minutes walk from the beach. The Sombrio area was heavily logged in the mid-1980s. An old route down to the shore through beautiful old-growth timber along the Sombrio River has been clearcut. A stand of trees was left on

A visitor is awed by the Red Creek Fir Tree.

the coastline, to bravely face the brunt of winter storms that at one time rolled over a sprawling forest of these aging veterans. Highlights of a visit to Sombrio Beach are the caves and waterfall found along the strand and the raw power and beauty of the sea.

Perhaps the worst hill on the gravel section of our run is an S-shaped corner known locally as Switchback Hill. No matter what the season, you can be sure this grade will be rutted and bumpy.

The gravel ends at km 60.3 (mi 37.5). In its approach to Port Renfrew, the road dips down another hill and levels off near the cutoff to the Red Creek Fir (km 71/mi 44). You might consider travelling the 12 km (7.5 mi) or so to the parking area and trailhead up to this ancient Douglas fir. Estimated as between 800 and 1,000 years old, the Red Creek Fir is Canada's largest known living Douglas fir, standing over 73 m (239 ft) high. The road in follows the bed of an old rail line.

There is a major junction at km 73.3 (mi 45.5). Straight ahead goes in through the Port Renfrew townsite and terminates near the government dock and the Port Renfrew Hotel. Cerantes Road, just before the hotel, winds in to Botanical Beach and the tidepools found there. (See **Trip 2**.) A right turn at the intersection leads travellers to the one-lane bridge over the San Juan River and the sandy beach on Port San Juan. There is a private wilderness campsite here operated by the local Indian band.

Some paddlers head up the San Juan River to Fairy Lake. This lower section of the river is tidal so it helps to be knowledgeable of the tides. The San Juan can be tricky. Fallen trees and rogue deadheads may impede progress. Currents in the vicinity of the constantly shifting sand and gravel bars can increase suddenly: in heavy rains the shift is dramatic; in late spring, the sun melting snows on the higher elevations produces a more gradual influence on the San Juan waters.

Where the road splits, West Coast Trail hikers will swing left to the southern terminus of this challenging route along the southwest coast of Vancouver Island. To the right leads visitors across a branch of the San Juan (via the Deering Bridge) to another junction.

A marina and RV park is now located on the banks of the Gordon River, at a site once used by Fletcher Challenge (formerly BCFP) crews. The entrance is about 1 km (0.6 mi) west of the Deering Bridge. Turn right at the bridge (following the Cowichan signpost) for the Fairy Lake campsite about 3 km (1.9 mi) along. Fairy Lake is a good place to base camp. From here you can day trip to area attractions. A detailed look at Fairy Lake and the backroads from Port Renfrew up to Cowichan Lake is featured in **Trip 4**.

Contacts:

Canadian Pacific Forest Products (Sooke) (604) 642-5237; Western Forest Products (Jordan River) (604) 646-2031; Ministry of Parks (Victoria) (604) 387-5002; Public Information Officer (604) 387-4609/387-3940; Ministry of Forests (Victoria) (604) 387-5255; Capital Regional District (Victoria) (604) 478-3344; Sooke Region Museum (Sooke) (604) 642-6112; Fletcher Challenge (Gordon River Camp) (604) 749-6881; Fletcher Challenge (Caycuse Division) (604) 745-3324.

Maps/Guides:

Hiking Trails Vol. I (Outdoor Club of Victoria); *Victoria in a Knapsack* (Sierra Club of B.C.); *Outdoor Recreation Map of B.C. No.15* (Greater Victoria-Gulf Islands-Nanaimo Region) (Outdoor Recreation Council of B.C.); *Visitors Guide to Renfrew, Cowichan and Nitinat* (Fletcher Challenge); *Guide to Forest Land of Southern Vancouver Island* (Lake Cowichan Combined Fire Organization); WFP Logging Road Map (Jordan River); Topographical Maps: 92C9 *Port Renfrew* (1:50,000); 92B5 *Sooke* (1:50,000); 92C8 *Jordan River* (1:50,000); 92B/NW *Victoria* (1:125,000); 92C/NE *Nitinat Lake* (1:125,000).

Nearest Services:

Western Communities; Sooke; Port Renfrew.

Trip 2: Botanical Beach

In Brief:

Botanical Beach, west of Port Renfrew, is renowned for its tidepools. At low tide, an expansive sandstone shelf is exposed revealing intertidal life within natural wave-carved pools. A marine biology station was once located here. Beachcombing, rock scrambling and the great seascapes attract countless visitors yearly.

Access:

Follow the West Coast Road (Hwy 14) to Port Renfrew. Turn left onto Cerantes Road near the Port Renfrew hotel and the government wharf. Cerantes Road is gravel and deteriorates as you near the beach. Early season washouts may require a four-by-four. There are a couple of roadside pulloffs for those choosing to hike in.

Description:

Botanical Beach is one stop most Port Renfrew visitors mark on their agenda. The tidepools on the sandstone shelf are exposed at low tide, revealing a variety of sea life within the natural bathtubs. The relative ease with which visitors may view the marine life is a big feature of the area.

The University of Minnesota established a marine biology laboratory on Botany Bay, at the turn of the last century. It was the first of its kind in North America. The facility was headed by Dr. Josephine Tilden, marine biologist at the University of Minnesota.

The lab operated from 1901 to 1906. At its peak, the seaside station had a kitchen, dining room, a lounge and the lab buildings. Eighty people could be housed at the site. Students and scientists from all over the world journeyed in to Botanical Beach to study its wealth of marine life.

The tidepools on the sandstone shelf at Botanical Beach harbour a variety of marine life.

Lack of funding coupled with the difficulty of bringing in supplies spelled doom for the station. The University of Minnesota did not come up with operating money. Supplies and people were brought in on *The Queen City*, a small steamer with a regular run to Port Renfrew at the time. Capricious west coast weather and treacherous seas made the service sporadic at best. Supplies landed in Port Renfrew then had to be lugged along an arduous trail to the laboratories.

It was not an easy task for those involved and it is somewhat surprising that the station operated for six years. Such was the perseverance and dedication of its participants — especially the efforts of Dr. Tilden. Several universities have studied marine life at Botanical Beach over the years, including the University of B.C. and the University of Victoria. During the Second World War, a gun emplacement was constructed on the shoreline near the beach. It was never used and later was dismantled.

To get to Botanical Beach, drive to Port Renfrew on the West Coast Road (Hwy 14). Go through the community to the sharp corner near the Port Renfrew Hotel and the government dock. Cerantes Road (just before the hotel) is the beach access road (see **Trip 1**).

It's an idea to drive out onto the government wharf (if there's not much activity on the pier) and take in the scenery of Port San Juan. Snuggery Cove, the small bay near the wharf, regularly bustles with the comings and goings of commercial fishing vessels, pleasure craft and smaller boats.

You might even be inclined to drop into the hotel for a little refreshment before tackling the sometimes-rough road to the beach access points. Pasted, taped and stapled on two walls in the hotel pub are countless dollar bills — many from hikers who have completed a trek along the West Coast Trail. (Port Renfrew is the southern terminus of this world-famous wilderness route). Some of the bills making up this monetary wallpaper carry written impressions from trail travellers; often quite humourous comments.

Once on Cerantes Road, you'll be heading southwest towards San Juan Point. If it's at all foggy during your visit, you'll hear the drone of the fog horn, south of the point in the vicinity of Cerantes Rock. On a clear day you'll be able to see across Port San Juan to the far shoreline. Hidden in the forest on this side of the bay, the first stretch of the West Coast Trail snakes its way west to Owen Point.

There are two hills along Cerantes Road that are prone to washouts and can be problem spots in the off-season. If you're in doubt as to whether or not your vehicle will make it in all the way, remember that you can always park your car on the roadside and hike in to the beach. There are several pulloffs on the way in. Not everyone likes to drive on rough roads.

There are two ways in to the beach area at Botanical. At km 3.2 (mi 2) the road splits. The route to the right deadends at a turnaround and parking area close to a short, root-filled and salal- bordered trail that drops sharply down to the north section of the beach. By keeping to the left road at the junction, you can drive to an area of logging, and park your car on the shoulder of the road, and hike down to the main beachfront, following a washed-out road. There is a third road at the junction, on the far left, which climbs a short hill right before it rejoins the main beach access road.

In the past, visitors would park on the knoll and hike about 15 minutes to the water. In 1987, logging was taking place near Botanical Beach, and a new logging road was pushed through, bypassing the old route. One washout was repaired and the old road was upgraded for truck access.

In the spring of 1988, negotiations were concluded between the provincial government and A-Team Industries Ltd. of Parksville (who were logging the area). The government acquired 243.8 hectares (602 acres) of land near Botanical Beach for a little over $300,000.

In the fall of 1983, 1.6 hectares (4 acres) of property in the area was obtained by the Nature Conservancy of Canada; with assistance from the Nature Trust and the W.J. Van Dusen Foundation (Vancouver). This tract of land was subsequently leased to the province on a 99-year term for a nominal fee.

When this parcel of property is added to the 1988 acquisition and the existing foreshore reserve, a total of 325 hectares (803 acres) is now in the government's hands. Plans were announced in March of 1988 that the Botanical Beach area was to be slated for provincial park status. Future plans

The headland is one of several geographical features of Botanical Beach.

include improved road access, trail maintenance and the construction of washrooms and an information centre.

There is much to see at Botanical Beach. Within the tidepools, anemones, starfish, large and small fish and plant life can easily and safely be observed at low tide. On a recent trip, a friend and I were fortunate enough to watch the foraging of a small octopus trapped in a deep pool near a rock cleft.

There are opportunities to witness the force of the Pacific Ocean as it angrily smashes its foaming seas onto the sandstone shelf and shoreline rocks. Some of the largest breakers I have ever seen lashed the storm-churned coast at Botanical one winter. Wind- driven and storm-derived, the combers surged pell-mell into the shoreline crags, tossing white spindrift high into the air.

Botanical Beach's topography is a challenge to the hiker and rock scrambler. You can traverse the shore between the two trail access points at low tide, passing a sheer headland en route. Anyone contemplating such a hike MUST have a clear knowledge of the tides. In many places, you could be trapped by the flood.

Tidal information is available in the Canadian Hydrographic Service publication, *Canadian Tide and Current Tables: Vol. 6*, available at marine supplier or most tackle and department stores.

One section of the sandstone shelf is known as The Devil's Billiard Table. Visitors are fascinated by its sea-carved bathtubs: some camouflaged by seaweed, and all containing a profusion of marine life. Some people will enjoy exploring nooks and crannies along the jagged beachfront; others will content themselves with the exceptional seascape — complete with passing fishing boats and freighters.

There is really no best time to visit Botanical Beach. Coinciding your foray with the lowest tides of the year (usually late June) makes good sense. I prefer the solitude the region offers over the winter months. It is during that time of year that some of the more spectacular storms lash the beach.

Whenever you do visit Botanical Beach, you're sure to get a taste of raw nature on Vancouver Island's west coast. Don't forget to consult the tidebooks for low tides so you can see as many of the unique tidepools as possible.

Contacts:

Ministry of Parks (Victoria) (604) 387-5002; Public Information Officer (Victoria) (604) 387-4609/387-3940; Sooke Region Museum (Sooke) (604) 642-6112.

Maps/Guides:

Hiking Trails Vol. 1 (Outdoor Club of Victoria); *Victoria In A Knapsack* (Sierra Club of B.C.); *Guide to Forest Land of Southern Vancouver Island*, (Lake Cowichan Combined Fire Organization); Topographical Maps: 92C9 *Port Renfrew* (1:50,000); 92C/NE *Nitinat Lake* (1:125,000).

Nearest Services:

Port Renfrew.

Trip 3: The Butler Mainline

In Brief:

The Butler Main logging road goes into the heart of the Sooke Hills. Stocked lakes (Tugwell, Ranger, Boulder and others) lure fishermen. Backroads explorers can drive along two B.C. Hydro reservoirs (Bear Creek and Diversion). A rugged loop drive through Leechtown is one option. West Leech Falls are impressive after heavy rains.

Access:

Follow Hwy 14 to Sooke. Turn right onto Otter Point Road and right again onto Young Lake Road. Butler Main begins near Camp Barnard (Boy Scout facility). The route is a gravel mainline with some steep hills and narrow sections. Secondary roads are rough and may require a four- by-four. These logging roads are restricted access routes.

Description:

One of the more popular backroading regions on the Lower Island is the area north of Sooke accessed by the Butler Main logging road. This mainline can be driven in a normal car; the spur roads generally require a high-slung vehicle or four-by-four. You can head up into the mountains to fishing lakes, swimming holes and scenic vistas.

In Sooke, turn right onto Otter Point Road. Turn right again onto Young Lake Road 4.7 km (3 mi) along. At the entrance to Camp Barnard, cut right onto Butler Main and set your odometer to 0. Just over 1 km along (0.6 mi), you can take Boneyard Main (signposted) and drive through a gravel pit and follow this route into Leechtown. Let's take a look at this backroads option.

Boneyard Lake is about 5 km (3 mi) from the pit. It's a popular spot

19

for summer swimmers. The road follows close by the Sooke River at one point and then turns to cross the bridge near the confluence of Golledge Creek and the Sooke River. At the top of the next hill, there is a roadside **pulloff**. By walking through the woods down to the river you will come upon a beautiful stretch of this waterway and some great potholes for swimming.

Near Leechtown, the road curves to the left and follows the Leech River Valley to eventually connect up with Butler Main. By keeping straight ahead and crossing the Leech River bridge, you can find the restricted road near a watchman's shack that goes in to MacDonald Lake. A side road on the **right** at the north end of the lake leads to some rustic picnic sites. MacDonald Lake can be productive for spring and fall fishermen.

If the water in the Sooke River is low, you have the option of fording a shallow section and then driving along the east side of Sooke Lake to hook up with the Shawnigan Lake South Road. This backroad passes through part of the Greater Victoria Water District and is a restricted area. No stopping or **leaving** your vehicle is permitted. This region is regularly patrolled by Water District employees.

Gold was discovered in the Leech River back in 1864. For a time, Leechtown and nearby Boulder City became gold boomtowns. Little remains of these settlements today. Currently, there are some mining claims in the vicinity of Valentine Mountain. Lone prospectors still sluice parts of the **Leech River**. Legends of Spanish treasure hidden in the hill abound; one story tells of a hidden gold cache arrived at by descending a series of carved stone steps on a montainside.

Let's return to the Boneyard cutoff on Butler Main, near the gravel pit. The mainline starts a climb east of Bluff and Trapp mountains. Around the 10.5 km (6.5 mi) mark keep an eye out for an old washed-out road on the left. You can hike up this overgrown roadbed to Tugwell Lake, one of the many stocked lakes in this area. A trail of sorts goes along the lake to many casting spots.

Tugwell Main intersects Butler Main at km 11.7 (mi 7.2). By turning left here and heading south, you'll come to Branch TW 40, which runs up to Ranger Lake. This branch road is suitable only for four-by- fours. Part way **up** you can see Tugwell Lake and are treated to an outstanding view of the surrounding mountains. Ranger Lake will appear on the right. There is a small roadside pulloff nearby. From here, a rocky trail winds down to an elevated rocky point at lakeside.

I've been up to Ranger Lake in the early spring, when the lake was still frozen over. Telltale signs of thaw were evident around the many logs jutting **out** from the lake's edge. As the sun palely beat down on Ranger, periodic snaps and rumblings echoed from the ice; pockets of trapped air escaped with a hissing sound each time the ice shifted.

One of the beauties of the Sooke Hills is that over the winter, even though there may be no snow in areas close to sea level, to find winter all you have to do is travel the backroads up above the snow line. There you'll have plenty of the white stuff.

The next spur road beyond TW 40 goes up to tiny Forslund Lake, little more than a pond to the north of Mount Muir. Again, this route is passable only by a four-by-four or all-terrain vehicle.

Butler Main passes a small lake (yet another good swimming spot in hot weather) before turning sharply to the west. Here you'll be treated to a lofty panorama of the Leech River Valley. If it's a clear day you'll be able to identify Mount Baker, over in Washington state. The only thing that detracts from the view is the clearcut logging on many of the nearby mountains.

The left turn for Boulder Lake is at km 14.4 (mi 9). There are two steep hills on the way in that could require a four-by-four. Parts of the road are usually rutted. At the crest of the second incline, Boulder Lake will be visible below the road to the right. It's easy to see how the lake got its name — many large rocks and boulders lie scattered in the waters and around the island in the centre. You might catch a glimpse of a lone eagle wheeling high above the western fringes of the trees on the lake's far side. Deer tracks are often seen at the lakeshore.

Anglers using small spinners are often successful at enticing a rainbow trout to strike. Fly fishermen also have good luck using tried and true flies such as the Royal Coachman or a shrimp imitation. A trail leads along the lake to numerous casting locations. A cartop boat or canoe will nicely complement a visit to Boulder Lake. You can follow an old logging road down to an area where wilderness campers can set up near the lake. Remember to pack out any garbage.

Beyond the Boulder Lake turn, at km 15 (mi 9.3), you'll reach the Leechtown/Boneyard road (on the right) on which you can journey east to Leechtown and loop down Boneyard Main back to the junction with Butler Main near the gravel pit. West Leech Main, as this artery is named, can be rough. It is pronc to washouts, especially one long, steep grade.

On one trip, a fellow backwoods browser and I came upon one rutted section where the roadbed had sagged towards the valley to our left; to our right, a deep gulley had been carved by runoff water in the shale and mud. The problem spot had been filled in somewhat by previous travellers using rocks, branches and nearby fragments of wood. We were able to gingerly get through.

In the early season, rain and melting snow can create havoc on unmaintained Island backroads. A friend and I encountered such conditions along West Leech Main one spring. It was quite a challenging route, even

An old flume snakes down the Jordan River valley.

though we were in his four-by-four. Trees lay toppled over, roots and all, having tumbled from their tenuous positions on the unstable hillside. Mudslides and rocks barred the roadway, and great gouges had been eaten out of the gravel by runoff streams.

A secondary road to Weeks Lake is on the right, just past the West Leech cutoff. Backroaders can journey in to Weeks Lake, Jarvis Lake and the Shawnigan/Renfrew Road. (See **Trip 5**.)

At this point, Butler Main heads west. At km 17 (mi 10.5) Valentine Main angles off to the right and up the east side of that mountain, towards Jordan Meadows. Bear Creek Reservoir, one of three B.C. Hydro water reserves providing for their Jordan River power- generating station, will be on your left by km 20 (mi 12.4). Watch for a side road going down to primitive campsites near the reservoir. This man-made lake was created in 1912 with the construction of an earthen dam at its west end.

Around the 24 km (15 mi) mark, look for the spur road (on the left) that will bring you to the Bear Creek bridge and down the road that skirts the south side of Diversion Reservoir. If you miss this turn, you'll end up at a locked gate farther down the mainline. It's about 5 km (3 mi) from this cutoff to Diversion Dam. This structure was completed in 1913. The third reservoir is further down the Jordan River Valley. Called the Elliot Reservoir, it was built between 1968 and 1971. Diversion Dam was scheduled for restrengthening beginning in the summer of 1989, as a safeguard against earthquake damage.

On the way to Diversion Dam, the road runs beside a short section of Jordan River. It's often jammed with deadheads that drift in from the reservoir. Occasionally, the stream is clear. That's the time to paddle up the river to the confluence with Bear Creek and on to a small falls. Paddlers should be aware of the floating logs in the reservoir. What was a clear launching spot in the morning could become choked with deadheads by late afternoon. I discovered that fact on a day outing on reservoir waters.

Being dammed, both Bear Creek and Diversion reservoirs harbour sunken stumps and branches that can be hazardous to paddlers. Water levels in the reservoirs fluctuate, depending on weather. At some times of the year, the stumps are well below the surface; in extremely dry conditions, they pose manoeuvring problems to anyone on the water. When the wind gets up, canoeists and kayakers should be wary. Along the road in to Diversion Dam, there are a couple of access points from which you can launch. In the summer, these are popular wilderness swimming holes.

Diversion Dam is an impressive sight and well worth the trip in to see. Water is released regularly through a large valve and makes for an amazing display as it cascades into the riverbed below.

The gravel road then turns south to follow the Jordan River Valley and down to the community of Jordan River. Active logging in this region now restricts public access, with a locked gate near Alligator Creek barring the route.

For those seeking a Lower Island backroad adventure, journeying along the Butler Main logging road and up into the Sooke Hills may just be what you're looking for.

Contacts:

Canadian Pacific Forest Products Ltd.(Sooke) (604) 642-5237; Western Forest Products Ltd. (WFP) (Jordan River) (604) 646-2031

Maps/Guides:

Outdoor Recreation Maps of B.C. No. 15 (Greater Victoria-Gulf Islands-Nanaimo Region) (Outdoor Recreation Council of B.C.); *Guide to Forest Land of Southern Vancouver Island*; Jordan River Road Map, (WFP); Topographical Maps: 92B5 *Sooke* (1:50,000); 92B12 *Shawnigan Lake* (1:50,000); 92B/NW *Victoria* (1:125,000)

Nearest Services:

Sooke

Trip 4: Port Renfrew to Cowichan Lake

In Brief:

This trip follows logging mainlines from Port Renfrew to Mesachie Lake, on the south shore of Cowichan Lake. Highlights are the Lizard Lake and Fairy Lake campsites, a giant spruce point of interest and the Harris Creek and Robertson River valleys. There is excellent mountain scenery although some hillsides bear the scars of poor logging practices from years gone by.

Access:

From Port Renfrew drive east to the Harris Creek 'Y.' Turn north and follow the signposts. There are stretches of pavement, though the route is mainly gravel with some steep hills. The road is restricted- access within Canadian Pacific Forest Products Ltd. territory.

Description:

We'll begin the backroads jaunt from the Port Renfrew area up to Cowichan Lake at the Deering Bridge over the San Juan River (see **Trip 1**). Once across the bridge, turn right at the signpost for Cowichan Lake. Mark this point as km/mi 0.

There are more narrow, wooden spans ahead that must be negotiated, the first at Fairy Creek. The entrance to the Fletcher Challenge Fairy Lake campsite is at km 3 (mi 1.9). There are many campsites here, spread along a winding, forested road that leads in to the lake. The site provides ample space for summer travellers and offers a quiet oasis of solitude for those journeying in the off-season.

The area was once homesteaded by Vander Waver, of Dutch origin. He discovered that rhubarb thrived in his garden and entered some samples at the Chicago World's Fair in 1933. His entry took first prize. In the late twenties, a religious commune was set up in the region. The Rainbow Farm, as it was called, was comprised of Stratford bible students. They obtained a land grant, set up buildings and dwellings, constructed a community hall, utilized heavy farm machinery and raised cattle. It was an idealistic dream. With the onset of monetary problems associated with the Great Depression, the commune closed down.

Lumbering has always been a primary industry of the district. The British Canadian Lumber Company (1912-1914) established a rail line from Fairy Lake to the mouth of the Gordon River. Other loggers of note were W.E. Cathel and C. Sorenson. Another logging railroad, originating near Harris Creek, ran along the southern banks of the San Juan River, also to the Gordon River.

Fairy Lake is fed by two streams: Fairy and Renfrew (Granite) creeks. Fairy Creek enters the lake near the shoreline campsites. A trail goes in to the creekmouth. Renfrew Creek pours into the lake's east side after tumbling its way down through the mountains northeast of Fairy Lake. A short outlet stream connects the lake with the San Juan River. Canoeists and boaters can head out into the river via this tree-lined waterway. Anyone spending time on the San Juan will notice the tidal effect on its waters. At high tide, the current is minimal, making for easy paddling. During an ebbing flow, the complexion of the San Juan changes. This can produce tricky currents and potentially hazardous waters for inexperienced paddlers. A good knowledge of the tides is essential for river runners.

The Fairy Lake campsite has running water and comfort stations. Firewood is available during the summer months. Over the winter, lower sections of the campground are prone to flooding from rising lake waters. There are two developed beach areas at Fairy Lake, each gently sloping down into the lake. One has a float anchored to the lake bottom. Used as a swimming and sunning platform by bathers in the summer, it often is a base of operation for spring and fall anglers using bait and bobber, lures and flyfishing gear. Some fishing restrictions apply to Fairy Lake. Between October 1 and April 30 of each year it is a "trout release" lake and only artificial flies may be used.

Beyond the Fairy Lake campsite entrance, the road skirts the lake's northern fringes and heads east to the Renfrew Creek bridge. Then comes the Harris Creek bridge at km 10.7 (mi 6.5). Two side roads on either end of this span drop down to the stream and some wilderness picnic sites.

A major junction is reached at km 12.8 (mi 8). Called the Harris Creek 'Y,' it is one of the best-known logging road intersections on Southern Vancouver Island. Here, we'll turn north for Cowichan Lake. Straight ahead used to connect with Shawnigan Lake. The Williams Creek suspension bridge

The diving platform at Lizard Lake is a lonely site when the seasons change.

was blocked off in 1987, as it was unsafe for vehicular traffic. For a description of the run east from Port Renfrew to this bridge, see **Trip 5**.

Just under 2 km (1.2 mi) along is the entrance to the Fletcher Challenge Lizard Lake campsite. This tiny locale is a favourite with Port Renfrew locals. There is a limited number of camping locations at Lizard and a boat launch. A diving platform, moored offshore, is used by swimmers. I've found good fishing action at the lake's east end. Locals have told me that sometimes the fish can be hard to catch due to the wide variety of food readily available to them in lake waters. You might mistake surfacing newts as fish sign — Lizard is full of them; hence its name.

North of Lizard Lake, the road, which is intermittent pavement up to this point, turns to gravel. At the 17.5 km (10.8 mi) mark of our run, the route crosses Harris Creek near the confluence of Harris and Hemmingsen creeks. To the right, as you cross the bridge, you'll see a deep canyon jutting upstream that is worth a look. Downstream is a deep pool often frequented by swimmers who must first scramble down the rocky bank to the river below. You can park on either side of the bridge. Make sure you're well off to the shoulder of the road. Steelheading is popular in many pools in the lower reaches of Harris Creek; however, a "No fishing" regulation is in place above and including Hemmingsen Creek. Anglers should check the fresh-

The giant spruce is a point of interest at the Old Harris Creek camp.

water fishing guide carefully before setting out.

Fletcher Challenge has signposted the giant spruce point of interest at km 20.2 (mi l2.5). Take a left turn onto the spur leading to the location of the former Harris Creek logging camp. This camp operated in the days of railway logging. The giant spruce is on display here. This butt log was cut down in 1958 along the San Juan River flats. That particular area was renowned for supplying airplane spruce for wartime production.

The mountainsides in this area reflect modern logging methods with most of the hilltops left intact with a crown of trees. This prevents some of the more serious erosion caused by runoff in the lower sections. The road follows Harris Creek with the stream right at roadside in a number of places. There are some great swimming holes in this stretch — usually at river bends where the current has gouged out deep pools in the riverbed. On days when the weather is scorching and the driving dusty, a quick dip in one of these natural bathtubs is a refreshing break. Two such pools are quite close together.

A water tower will be visible on the right and then a signpost marking the right turn for Cowichan Lake. At this point, you'll be leaving Fletcher Challenge woodlands and entering Canadian Pacific Forest Products Ltd. territory. This section of the route passes through active logging areas and regions where hauling is taking place, so it's best to tackle this part of the run after weekday working hours.

A steep hill is encountered next and you'll switchback up the mountainside. From a high vantage spot you'll see a stark display on the hills. Denuded of trees, the peaks have been ravaged over time by wind and rain: the bare, rocky summits are graphic evidence of the consequences of early logging practices and a devasting forest fire in the 1950s.

Eventually the road descends into the Robertson River Valley and levels out substantially. You'll drive through the Canadian Pacific logging yard and reach the South Shore Road at Mesachie Lake, where there is a flashing amber light. At this intersection, you can turn right for the village of Lake Cowichan; or you can turn left to follow the logging road along Cowichan Lake's south side for more backwoods browsing. That choice is up to you.

Contacts:

Fletcher Challenge (Gordon River Camp) (604) 749-6881; Fletcher Challenge (Caycuse Camp) (604) 745-3324; Canadian Pacific Forest Products Ltd. (Lake Cowichan) (604) 749-3796

Maps/Guides:

Renfrew, Cowichan, and Nitinat Visitors Guide, (Fletcher Challenge); *Guide to Forest Land of Southern Vancouver Island*; Topographical Maps: 92C9 *Port Renfrew* (1:50,000); 92C16 *Cowichan Lake* (1:50,000); 92C/NE *Nitinat Lake* (1:125,000)

Nearest Services:

Port Renfrew; Mesachie Lake; Honeymoon Bay; Lake Cowichan

Trip 5: Shawnigan Lake to Port Renfrew

In Brief:

Up until late 1987, you could drive from Shawnigan Lake to Port Renfrew on the backroads. Then the Bedspring Suspension Bridge over Williams Creek was blocked off as it was found to be unsafe for vehicular traffic. This curving span is still worth a look. Whether you journey in from the east or west, you'll still find fishing lakes, riverside picnic sites and several wilderness campsites.

Access:

From the east: take Shawnigan Lake cutoff in Mill Bay from Highway 1 to the north end of the lake. Continue west onto the Port Renfrew road and follow the signs.

From the west: from Port Renfrew follow the logging road that runs east to the Harris Creek 'Y.' Keep straight ahead on the mainline. Roads are gravel with rough sections. Unmaintained sections may require a four-by-four. These roads are combined-use arteries in some areas.

Description:

This trip is divided into two parts: east and west.

East: Shawnigan Lake to the Bedspring Suspension Bridge.

The starting point for this part of the run is at the junction of Shawnigan Lake West Road and the Renfrew Road. You can turn off Highway 1 at the Shawnigan Lake South cutoff and reach this point; or you can take the Shawnigan Lake turn in Mill Bay.

From Mill Bay, it's 5.3 km (3.2 mi) to Shawnigan Lake village where you turn right. Go left near Mason's Beach and round the north end of Shawnigan Lake. Just over the 10 km (0.6 mi) mark, you'll reach the intersection with Shawnigan Lake West Road. Set your odometer to 0 at this point.

Nearby is a signpost informing travellers about the Williams Creek bridge closure. Around 2 km (1 mi) along is Glen Eagle Road. By turning right here and following this gravel road you can find the old railway right-of-way leading in to the Kinsol trestle. Park at the top of a sharp hill and hike in. The former trackbed is to the right. There are a number of private residences nearby so respect each homeowner's privacy.

This short walk goes north to the trestle which was once part of a Canadian National Railway line. Both ends of the trestle are barricaded and signs warn against walking on the span — it's unsafe. The old bridge crosses the wide Koksilah River Valley. You can scramble down to the river via a rough trail and reach fishing and picnicking locations.

In the summer of 1988, someone foolishly lit a fire on the trestle that burned a large section and posed quite a problem for firefighters. There has been talk of restoring the wooden structure as part of a linear park. The bane of the plan — lack of funding — continues to delay any such development.

West of Gleneagle Road, the pavement ends. At km 5.2 (mi 3.2) is the Burnt Bridge turn. The Renfrew Road veers left to climb a small hill. By turning right and crossing the Koksilah River, you'll be entering Koksilah River Provincial Park, established in 1957. There are numerous roads through this wilderness park: side roads descend to riverside deadends; one cliff-hugs its way up the valley; another goes into the hills south of the Koksilah Ridge.

The Renfrew Road follows the south side of the Koksilah River. This is a picturesque stretch, especially when the Koksilah is running high. Another tiny section of Koksilah Provincial Park is ahead. It's identifiable by a wide pulloff on the right hand side of the road. Short trails lead in to some forested picnic sites.

A little farther along, the road forks. To the left is an active and restricted access logging road (signposted). Keep right at this point to follow the public road. A long grade begins. At the top is a fine view across a deep valley over to Mount Lazar. During the winter, snows may choke this stretch of road rendering it impassable for a time.

A somewhat confusing intersection is reached at the bottom of the long hill. There are many logging roads in the vicinity and some are not clearly marked on some maps. The Renfrew Road is signposted at some of the junctions, though the signs are small and sometimes hard to pick out. When in doubt, it's best to keep going straight ahead.

The Weeks Lake cutoff is at km 19.3 (mi 12). The Renfrew Road crosses two small bridges before this turn. Go left onto a secondary road for Weeks. At a fork in the road, go left again; to the right is a restricted-access area. Soon after passing a gravel pit (on the left) the access road for Weeks

The Bedspring Suspension Bridge over Williams Creek was once a thrill to drive across. The span has now been closed to traffic.

Lake and the natural boat launch on its shores will be visible. There are a couple of wilderness campsites nearby.

The Weeks Lake Road continues along the east side of the lake to hook up with the Butler Main, north of Sooke. This route can be rough, especially in the early season, but at certain times of the year you can loop through to Sooke without a four-wheeler. During the fire season you may find a gate along the way is locked. Weeks is regularly stocked with fish and is a popular destination for anglers. It's also an excellent paddling lake.

Just south of Weeks is an hourglass-shaped pond surrounded by tall trees. A trail leads in to this body of water. You can easily portage a canoe in, although there could be some deadfalls to climb over. By hiking up some of the old washed-out spur roads near Weeks Lake, you will find viewpoints looking down over the lake and out to the surrounding mountains. Some of the slopes display the stark evidence of clearcut logging.

Back on the Renfrew Road, the route runs through a narrow pass directly south of Mount Todd. Ahead, in the Clapp Creek region, North San Juan Main cuts off the Renfrew Road, to the right; South San Juan Main runs to the left. Both of these active arteries have gates near the cutoffs so they're easy to recognize. The next bridge is at Floodwood Creek, where the road dips down a small grade. There are a couple of creekside pulloffs that make for good rest stops to stretch your legs or indulge in a streamside picnic.

Around the 31 km (19 mi) mark is a favourite point of interest for many backwoods browsers: the Bedspring Suspension Bridge over the rocky cleft of Williams Creek. It is here that the Renfrew Road is blocked off.

The curving bridge used to give quite the thrill to travellers. You wouldn't see the span until you were right upon it. It appeared that the road dropped off into oblivion as you neared the approach. The gorge below the bridge is almost 45 m (150 ft) deep. This wooden plank bridge is supported by six massive cables attached to buried anchor logs on either side of the ravine. One section has a tension device built in. Four additional cables stretch out from the sides of the span to connect to stumps on the canyon walls. These prevented side-motion and sway. As it was, there was still a fair amount of bridge movement with each passing vehicle.

You may no longer be able to drive on the suspension bridge; yet this bridge is one reason the backroads from Shawnigan Lake west to Williams Creek still see their share of backwoods browsers.

West: Port Renfrew to the Bedspring Suspension Bridge.

This backroads jaunt begins at the Deering Bridge over the north branch of the San Juan River, just outside Port Renfrew. (See **Trip 1**.) Turn right at the north end of the bridge and follow the signs for Cowichan Lake. The road skirts the north end of Fairy Lake. Fletcher Challenge's Fairy Lake campsite is a popular camping destination. (For a detailed peek at this facility, see **Trip 4**.)

Keep right at the Harris Creek "Y" at km 12.8 (mi 8). To the left the road snakes up to Mesachie Lake on the south side of Cowichan Lake. (See **Trip 4**.) At km 15.2 (mi 9.4) is the intersection with the south end of the Lens Creek logging road. This mainline follows the Lens Creek Valley and hooks into the Port Renfrew/Cowichan Lake road farther north. The gates along this route are normally locked due to active logging. The Pixie Lake access road is a short distance up Lens Creek Main. You can drive in to the lakeside and launch a boat or canoe and attempt some trout fishing.

At the 17.4 km mark (10.8 mi) east of the Deering Bridge is the Fletcher Challenge wilderness campsite near the Black Suspension Bridge over the San Juan River. There are six sites at this user-maintained location. Anglers frequent the river pools during the steelhead season. Some outdoorsmen will launch boats from here and drift down to Fairy Lake. It can be a tricky undertaking. Some friends of mine like to start at the mouth of the San Juan River and canoe up to the campsite. One time they rescued two paddlers who had dumped in a treacherous chute on the waterway.

The Black Suspension Bridge is a treat to see. Camera buffs will delight at the photo opportunities of the river and bridge. This structure was also found to be unsafe for travel, so, like the Williams Creek span, it was

The Black Suspension Bridge over the San Juan River, east of Port Renfrew.

barricaded. A new bridge crosses the San Juan just upstream.

You might see a black bear in the vicinity of the switchback at Three Rivers Creek or the Sam Creek bridge. A friend and I once spotted a young cub foraging in the roadside fireweed. We stopped our car and cut the engine to observe the young animal. We didn't leave our vehicle; although we didn't see her, mother bear was no doubt nearby. A passing truck then sent the juvenile bear scurrying into thick underbrush.

There are many spur roads jutting off the Renfrew Road: Garbage Creek Main; Three Rivers Main; Dent Creek Main; Allan, Sam and Cedar Creek mainlines. These go into active logging areas or regions where cutting has already taken place.

Around the 30-km (18.5-mi) mark from our starting point is the switchback at Bear Creek. (This stream is called Blakeney Creek on some maps.) A heavy washout in 1982 swept away the road bridge at this location. Due to lumber slow downs at that time, little was done initially to repair the damaged bridge. It was eventually replaced, yet you can still see the effects of the washout on the grade leading down to the newer crossing. This hill can still be rough.

Back in 1982, I was journeying from Shawnigan Lake to Port Renfrew and, noting the severe condition of the road, I parked at the top of the hill on the east side of Bear Creek, and walked down to the former bridge site.

Massive timbers were strewn along the roadside and huge boulders blocked the route down. At the bottom, a man and his son were talking with a logging-company employee. The logger had just pulled the man's Volkswagen van out of the creekbed where it had become stuck in a futile attempt to cross the stream on a makeshift plank bridge. Apparently the travellers had been stuck there for twelve hours! The logger and I were the only people the man had seen since his vehicle had become stranded. This tale reflects the dangers of attempting too much in your vehicle on Island backroads. Common sense is applicable anywhere. When in doubt, turn around. One winter, I was following this backroad from Renfrew to Shawnigan Lake only to be halted at Bear Creek. Rather than rip off my car's exhaust system on the rocky hill beyond what was then the newly constructed bridge, I decided to retreat back to Port Renfrew.

The Bedspring Suspension Bridge is 7.5 km (4.5 mi) from Bear Creek. In this area there are many overgrown side roads that provide foot access to San Juan River canyons, pools and some blown trestles.

Despite the closure of the Williams Creek bridge, there are still plenty of things to see on the road east from Port Renfrew to this span.

Contacts:

Fletcher Challenge Ltd. (Gordon River Camp) (604) 749-6881; MacMillan Bloedel (Cowichan Woodlands Division) (604) 246-4714; B.C. Forest Service (Duncan) (604) 746-5123.

Maps/Guides:

Visitors Guide to Renfrew, Cowichan and Nitinat, (Fletcher Challenge); *Guide to Forest Land of Southern Vancouver Island; Outdoor Recreation Maps of B.C. No. 15* (Greater Victoria-Gulf Islands-Nanaimo Region), (Outdoor Recreation Council of B.C.); *Logging Road Guide to the Cowichan Division*, (MacMillan Bloedel); Topographical maps: 92C9 *Port Renfrew* (1:50,000); 92B12 *Shawnigan Lake* (1:50,000); 92C/NE *Nitinat Lake* (1:125,000); 92B/NW *Victoria* (1:125,000).

Nearest Services:

Port Renfrew; Shawnigan Lake.

Trip 6: The Backway to Cowichan Lake

In Brief:

Instead of taking Highway 18 from Duncan to the village of Lake Cowichan there is an alternate route. Follow the backroads which wend along the north side of the Cowichan River. The Skutz Falls area is one highlight and you'll view some Cowichan Valley scenery you might otherwise miss.

Access:

From Highway 1 in Duncan turn west onto Trunk Road. Trunk becomes Government. Turn left onto Gibbons Road to Menzies. Keep straight on Barnjum and then turn left onto Riverbottom Road. Route is paved most of the way. There are some sharp corners and gravel stretches can be bumpy with hills.

Description:

The usual route travellers take to Cowichan Lake is the 30-km (18.6-mi) drive down Highway 18, starting just north of the city of Duncan. This modern, paved artery runs through a demonstration forest and passes several lookouts along the way. Some visitors prefer the slower backway that meanders along the north side of the Cowichan River.

First you must find Riverbottom Road. In Duncan, turn west onto Trunk Road at the first set of traffic lights north of the silver bridge over the Cowichan River. Trunk Road becomes Government and then climbs a hill. Turn left onto Gibbons Road (near the hospital signpost) and continue to the intersection with Menzies Road. Go straight onto the gravel road — now called Barnjum. This runs into Riverbottom Road near Wake Lake. Turn left here.

Winter steelheaders are very familiar with this first stretch of the backroute; and during the steelhead season, drift boats are common on the

Skutz Falls is found along the backroads to Cowichan Lake.

Cowichan River. There are many river access points along Riverbottom Road. The road twists and turns to pass Stoltz Road and some logged-off patches of woodland. Then comes a steep hill indicating the Marie Canyon region.

The B.C. Forest Service has established a tiny recreation site overlooking the precipitous canyon. An abrupt stairway drops down to the river here. Take care when viewing the gorge from the cliffside paths — the forest floor can be slippery.

The road eventually drops down a hill and crosses a rail line. Two B.C. Forest Service wilderness campsites are in this vicinity. The Lower Skutz Falls site can be reached by making an immediate left turn once across the tracks. The upper location is closer to the falls, just beyond Mayo Road.

There are many riverside trails to follow; on one you can follow part of the Cowichan River Footpath (see **Trip 9**) and loop back to the Skutz Falls campsite. You won't see the well-known suspension footbridge that once spanned the Cowichan River east of the falls; it has been removed and replaced by a Forest Service road bridge.

The road veers away from the river and goes north toward Highway 18. A little before that junction, a rough road on the left will be seen. This leads back down to the river and more fishing pools. Parts of this road are best suited for four-by-fours.

Right before the Highway 18 intersection is Old Lake Cowichan Road. Turn left here and follow this backroad the rest of the way to the village of Lake Cowichan. The upper end of the Cowichan River Footpath emerges onto this road about 3 km (1.8 mi) from the townsite. Once in town, you can return to Duncan on the main highway or retrace your steps on the backroads.

Contacts:

B.C. Forest Service (Duncan) (604) 746-5123.

Maps/Guides:

Hiking Trails Vol. II, (Outdoor Club of Victoria); *Guide to Forest Land of Southern Vancouver Island*; Duncan City Map; Topographical Maps: 92B3 *Duncan* (1:50,000); 92C16 *Cowichan Lake* (1:50,000); 92B/NW *Victoria* (1:125,000); 92C/NE *Nitinat Lake* (1:125,000).

Nearest Services:

Duncan; Lake Cowichan.

Trip 7: Mount Prevost Memorial Park

In Brief:

Mount Prevost Memorial Park is located atop Mount Prevost, just north of the city of Duncan. The view from the 786 m (2578 ft) summit on a clear day takes in the Gulf Islands, Haro Strait, the city of Duncan and neighbouring parts of the Cowichan Valley. Many trails are found near the viewpoint. It's a great destination for a picnic in the sky.

Access:

From Highway 1 take Lake Cowichan Highway (Hwy 18) west to Somenos Road. Turn right and continue to Mount Prevost Road and the park signpost. Go left and begin the climb to the parking area. Road is gravel and narrow with steep sections. Logging along the road could restrict access.

Description:

Mount Prevost Memorial Park was officially opened on Remembrance Day in 1982. It evolved as a joint effort of the Royal Canadian Legion (Branch 53) and the Corporation of the District of North Cowichan. The project was initiated by Mrs. Prue C. Power. A memorial cairn was constructed on Mount Prevost in 1929, commemorating those from the Cowichan Valley who fell in WWI. Later, names of WWII casualties were added to the marker's bronze plaque. The 10-metre-high cairn (33 ft) is a Duncan landmark.

It's a 7.2 km (4.5 mi) drive to the parking area, and quite the climb on the constricted gravel roadway. There are a couple of viewpoints along the way.

Avid hikers can utilize Branch C or E to follow game trails to the top. Where the main road forks, keep left. From the parking area, a steep grade goes up to the war memorial — and one of the best viewpoints on Lower Vancouver Island. Extreme caution is recommended when walking near the

A visitor takes in the spectacular vista from atop Mount Prevost.

bluff. There are some environmentally sensitive areas atop Mount Prevost, notably a patch of wild, yellow fawn lilies. Keep to the trails at all times to help minimize damage to these fragile sections.

The road up can be a challenge during the rainy season and impassable in times of heavy snow. Logging may restrict weekday travel.

Contacts:

The Corporation of the District of North Cowichan (604) 746-7101; B.C. Forest Service (Duncan) (604) 746-5123.

Maps/Guides:

Hiking Trails Vol.II, (Outdoor Club of Victoria); *Guide to Forest Land of Southern Vancouver Island*; Duncan City Map; Topographical Maps: 92B3 *Duncan* (1:50,000); 92B/NW *Victoria* (1:125,000).

Nearest Services:

Duncan Area.

Trip 8: The Cowichan River Footpath

In Brief:

The Cowichan River Footpath begins just outside the city of Duncan and meanders along the banks of the Cowichan River, almost to the village of Lake Cowichan. It was originally a fishermen's trail; however, upgrading over the past two decades has turned the footpath into a fine day hiking area and a challenge for those hikers preferring to walk the complete length (30 km/18 mi). Wilderness campsites along the trail are numerous. Skutz Falls is one highlight as is the Marie Canyon area.

Access:

In Duncan take Allenby Road to the white bridge over the Cowichan River. Follow Indian Road to Glenora Road. From Glenora Road cut onto Vaux Road (which becomes Robertson) to the Cowichan Fish and Game Club. Parking is nearby. Roads are mostly paved with some gravel.

Description:

I am always surprised by the lack of people I encounter on walks along the Cowichan River Footpath. Sure, you'll run into visitors in the Skutz Falls area — that section is easily accessible by road — yet along much of the trail, you'll be alone. The footpath runs fron Glenora (near Duncan) almost to the village of Lake Cowichan, and follows the scenic splendour of the Cowichan River and surrounding forest. It's a 30 km (18 mi) trek.

Between 1960 and 1969, the Cowichan Fish and Game Association, in conjunction with the Victoria club, the provincial government, private companies and interested individuals, constructed and improved the foot trail. It took nine years to complete — partly because much of the work was undertaken by volunteers; partly due to the time and paperwork involved in gaining public access through privately-owned lands.

*The Cowichan River footpath
winds along the Cowichan River.*

The trail passes through Crown land, Indian territory, private sectors and tracts of MacMillan Bloedel property. Hikers should respect any notices on private land and Indian reserves. Co-operation created the footpath and the same degree of co-operation among its users and landowners should be maintained. Both the Cowichan and Victoria Fish and Game associations encourage people not to trespass on private sectors. This will guarantee continued public access along parts of the river. A major reason for the trail was to help fishermen get in to favourite river angling spots. In the past, many anglers would split their waders as they tramped upriver.

The Cowichan River was once called the gateway to Cowichan Lake. Log drives were common on its waters at the turn of the century. Some logs that were lost on the drives can still be identified along sections of the trail. Telltale marks of hand logging can be spotted in older stumps passed by hikers. The river is used by several canoe and kayak clubs at certain times of the year. There are countless swimming holes and picnic sites on both the north and south shores of the river. Access is easier from the north side where many roads lead in to riverside locations. Private cabins nestle in the woods along the lower sections of the Cowichan.

Beginning near the Fish and Game clubhouse, the trail first goes up a hill and down a gravel road to a junction. Turn right here and follow the blue and white trail markers to the river. The first view of the Cowichan River is near Holt Creek where you'll hit a steep incline. At the top is a viewpoint looking down into the gorge occupied by this small stream.

The first section of the footpath is easy for most visitors, wide and not excessively trying. It's a good day-hiking destination. Stump and Rickie-Dickie bridges cross potential wet areas. Most spans on the trail are signposted: named after various volunteers and Fish and Game Club members who assisted in the trail's construction.

A few years ago, on a jaunt along the full length of the footpath, a friend and I came upon a patch of stinging nettles in the first part of the route. We were both wearing shorts. We quickly increased our pace and surged through, voicing our displeasure.

At Carson's Corner there is a sheer clay bank on the river's north shore. Over the summer, this area is a favourite spot for river runners on inner tubes. A short distance along is the Camscot Wilderness Campsite, one of the trail's better camping regions.

While some landowners on whose property the trail passes have granted public passage, others have exercised their right to privacy. At one point, the trail cuts away from the river to follow the old CNR tracks before it re-enters the woods. It can be repetitive and uninspiring walking on the railway ties. Macy's Mud Hole — with all the prerequisites to live up to its name — and Fall-Off Bridge are right before Davie Corner, a good swimming and picnicking site. Then comes the Stoltz recreation area.

By taking the trail from Glenora to Lake Cowichan, you'll be hiking upstream and climbing most of the way. In dry weather, water levels in the Cowichan will be low. That's the time astute anglers will scout out various river pools and pick out likely fishy spots for the winter steelhead season. Brown, rainbow and cutthroat trout reside in the Cowichan. Current fishing regulations should always be checked by those planning a fishing excursion.

High cliffs loom into view as you approach the Marie Canyon region. You'll cross the Helen D. Watts Memorial Bridge, the longest wood-plank span on the trail, and then ascend another steep hill. A viewpoint at the top looks down over the rugged bank to a deep river pool. This is a good place for a snack or lunch break. Just ahead is the Mile 66.2 CNR trestle, high above the river. Then comes the steepest grade on the hike: the climb up the lofty sand and gravel bank near Horseshoe Bend.

I had the opportunity to talk with one of the trail planners who told me the story of the time that he and some workers were marking the route over the hill near the bend. They had spotted a lone angler working a riffle in the river far below the gravel bank. The fisherman had waded three-quarters of the way across the Cowichan in his steelheading effort. As the water had been crystal-clear at the time, the workers were also able to see two steelhead swimming upstream.

"The fish must have detected him somehow, because they suddenly veered over to hug the bank and continued upriver right by the angler who remained completely oblivious to their passing," the planner remarked.

The footpath crosses to the Cowichan's north side via a Forest Service bridge near Skutz Falls. At this point, you will have journeyed 19 km (11.5 mi). This bridge gives small lumber contractors a road connection with the woodlands on the Cowichan's south side. Negotiations to secure entry through private lands proved fruitless; so rather than disturb the river to any degree, the Forest Service removed the suspension footbridge and utilized existing foundations for the new road span. With the removal of the suspension bridge, a highlight of a hike along the footpath is now history. The Skutz Falls area can easily be reached by road. Two B.C. Forest Service campsites are nearby. This can be a busy place, especially on weekends.

The footpath continues along the river's north bank. Sometime in the 1970s, logging was done right down to the riverside, obliterating the trail in spots. Natural washouts also occurred during spring runoff. The trail was sometimes hard to locate in this area. In October of 1988, volunteers from the Outdoor Club of Victoria and the Duncan Sierra Club cleared overgrown sections and re-flagged parts of the route.

As you near the Mile 71 CNR trestle, your trek will almost be complete. Cabins will be visible on the river's south side and then the trail will wind away from the Cowichan and head up to Old Lake Cowichan Road, a short distance to the east of Lake Cowichan village. If you're planning on hiking the complete trail, it's an idea to park your vehicle at one end and arrange with a friend to drop you off at the other. That way, you can hike out and have your car waiting for you.

The Cowichan River Footpath dangles at times on weathered precipices, looks down into canyons cut through sheer rock, skirts rushing rapids and meanders through preaceful stands of timber carpeted by a fern floor. It's a hiker's gateway to the Cowichan Valley along the banks of the Island's most famous river: the Cowichan.

Contacts:

B.C. Forest Service (Duncan) (604) 746-5123.

Maps/Guides:

Cowichan Fish & Game Association Map; Haig-Brown Flyfishing Association River Map (anglers guide); *Hiking Trails Vol. II*, (Outdoor Club of Victoria); *Guide to Forest Land of Southern Vancouver Island*; Topographical Maps: 92B3 *Duncan* (1:50,000); 92C16 *Cowichan Lake* (1:50,000); 92B/NW *Victoria* (1:125,000).

Nearest Services:

Duncan; Lake Cowichan.

Trip 9: Cowichan Lake Loop Drive

In Brief:

One of the more popular regions on the Lower Island is the Cowichan Lake area. Ideal for a countless number of outdoor pursuits, the lake can be circled — partly on paved roads; partly on logging mainlines. You can chose from fully-serviced campgrounds to primitive camping spots. Paddlers will find many access points all around the lake.

Access:

From Highway 1 just north of Duncan turn onto Highway 18 and drive 30 km (18.6 mi) west to the village of Lake Cowichan. This trip follows paved roads and combined-use gravel mainlines. Secondary roads may be rough.

Description:

Over the summer months, the Cowichan Lake area is one of the most popular outdoor regions on southern Vancouver Island; yet even in the off-season, the thin plumes of blue smoke rising above the trees at one of many wilderness lakeside campsites reveal the presence of campers.

Starting in the community of Lake Cowichan, a 75-km (46-mi) loop drive can be made around Cowichan Lake: half on hardtop roads; the remainder on combined-use logging mainlines. Some travellers may prefer to locate near the paved roads, within easy access of serviced campsites and private resorts. The more adventurous will be drawn to the wilderness locales by the lure of logging-road exploration. Whatever your preference, it's probably close to a fishing hotspot.

Over 100 km (62 mi) of shoreline makes Cowichan Lake an excellent cruising or paddling lake. Power boaters and cartoppers piloted by anglers on extended creekmouth forays mingle with canoeists and kayakers on lake waters. Cowichan Lake is a large body of water and is susceptible to winds

44

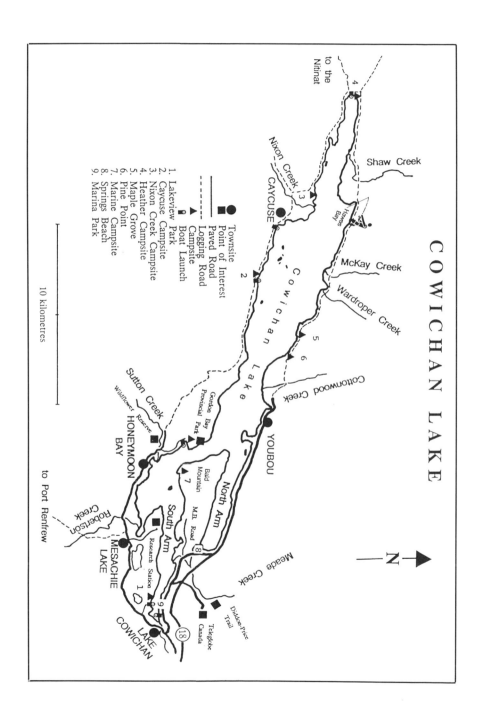

COWICHAN LAKE

to the
Nitinat

Shaw Creek

Nixon Creek
CAYCUSE

McKay Creek

Wardroper Creek

Cowichan Lake

Cottonwood Creek

Hawes Bay

Sutton Creek

Wildflower Reserve

HONEYMOON BAY

Gordon Bay Provincial Park

YOUBOU

North Arm

Bald Mountain
M.R. Road

Meade Creek

to Port Renfrew

Robertson Creek

MESACHIE LAKE

South Arm

Research Station

Diddup-Price Trail

Teleglobe Canada

LAKE COWICHAN

18

N →

Townsite
Point of Interest
Paved Road
Logging Road
Campsite
Boat Launch

1. Lakeview Park
2. Caycuse Campsite
3. Nixon Creek Campsite
4. Heather Campsite
5. Maple Grove
6. Pine Point
7. Marine Campsite
8. Springs Beach
9. Marina Park

10 kilometres

and the resultant wave action. The winds can come up surprisingly quickly, transforming rippled waters into a frenzy of whitecaps. It pays to be cautious and up to date on current weather information.

We'll begin our run in the village of Lake Cowichan. Located on the east side of Cowichan's South Arm, this community is 30 km (18.6 mi) west of Duncan. Set your odometer to 0 at the bridge over the Cowichan River, near the Riverside Inn. You'll now be on the South Shore Road.

At km 2 (mi 1.2) you'll reach the entrance to Lakeview Park, a semi-wilderness campground operated by the Lake Cowichan Parks Committee. A daily fee is charged, with firewood included. A club, affiliated with the Canadian Water Ski Association, sits adjacent to Lakeview Park.

The village of Mesachie Lake, 6 km (3.7 mi) west of Lake Cowichan townsite is home to the Cowichan Lake Forestry Research Station. This research facility, situated at the end of Forestry Road, offers group tours over the summer months. Here, visitors can see the province's main centre for genetic tree research, seed orchards and tree-improvement projects. The world's largest Douglas fir breeding plantations are nearby. The station was established in 1929, on Cowichan Lake's South Arm, with a second plot of land on the north shore added later. A bunkhouse and cookhouse dating back to the 1940s are now heritage buildings.

A left turn at the flashing amber light in Mesachie Lake will lead backwoods browsers south along the backroads into the Port Renfrew area. This is a restricted-access artery through Canadian Pacific Forest Products Ltd. territory south of Cowichan Lake. It is open to the public between 5 p.m. and 6 a.m. weekdays; all day on weekends and holidays. A run along this backroad from Port Renfrew to Cowichan Lake is covered in **Trip 4**.

Honeymoon Bay is around 4 km (2.5 mi) from Mesachie Lake The March Meadows Golf Course and a private RV park attract visitors as does Gordon Bay Provincial Park, on Walton Road. This campground is a favourite family-camping destination. Children return home with summer memories of swimming, boating and mountain hiking. One trail, beginning at the beach parking lot, goes up to an abandoned copper mine. The route follows an old road which is passable (when the gate is open) in a normal car for part of the way up.

There are decaying remains of mine workings to see and one side road leads in to a mine entrance. The shaft was sealed by Fletcher Challenge a few years ago for public safety reasons. On the way up are several expansive views of Cowichan Lake, looking north to Youbou and Saseenos Point.

Gordon Bay Park has 130 campsites, 16 of which are double units. An added feature is the boat launch which is suitable for larger boats. Other facilities include: heated washrooms, supplied firewood, a sani-station for trailers and RVs, public telephones and a visitor programme over the summer. There are also hot showers — welcome relief after a hot day's hike on area trails. A fee is charged from April to October. Gordon Bay Park is close to many North and South Arm fishing holes. A B.C. Forest Service marine park, located across the bay in the shadow of Bald Mountain, lures many boaters.

The Honeymoon Bay Wildflower Reserve is 1 km (0.6 mi) west of the Walton Road cutoff. Among the many rare species of wildflowers that grow here is the world's largest known concentration of pink fawn lilies. Other strange-named plants include False Solomon's Seal, Enchanter's Nightshade, Toothwart and Baneberry. Late spring is the best time to visit the reserve.

Right beyond the wildflower reserve, the gravel logging road section of the Cowichan Lake loop tour begins. We'll note this as km/mi 0 of our exploration of Cowichan Lake backroads.

The Fletcher Challenge Caycuse Campground is at km 9.8 (mi 6.0) and is another popular family campground. There are 27 sites to choose from. The preferred locations are along the lakefront. Other camping spots are situated along a forested road. There is a loop trail that will intrigue woodland explorers and the covered outdoor barbeque pit is a favourite with summer chefs. There is also a boat launch. The Caycuse Campground is just east of the logging community of Caycuse. During the week, it's not uncommon to see Fletcher Challenge tugs working the log booms out in Cowichan Lake. Some offshore islands near the campsite were once used as a burial ground by the Nitinaht Indians. Fishermen often troll around these islands. In fact, some of Cowichan Lake's hottest fishing locales are around the many lake islands and creekmouths.

Backwoods browsers used to drive right through the heart of Caycuse, at km 15 (mi 9.3); a bypass road now skirts the work yards. You can stop at the Fletcher Challenge Caycuse office and pick up a copy of their *Renfrew, Cowichan and Nitinat Visitor's Guide*: a good brochure to have with you, giving concise information on the region's camping, fishing and hunting. It describes many points of interest and offers a background on the region's forestry. There is a public boat launch and telephone in Caycuse.

The logging road heads due west as you leave Caycuse. Right before the Nixon Creek bridge is the Caycuse Seed Orchard, one of British Columbia's first industrial orchards. On the far side of the bridge (km 16/mi 10), the South Shore Road curves sharply to the right; straight ahead is a mainline going into the Gordon River logging camp.

The B.C. Forest Service Nixon Creek wilderness campsite sits on a picturesque bay, right around the corner from Nixon Creek. This tiny campground is user-maintained, so remember to tidy up when you leave. I first visited this Forest Service location when the access road from the logging mainline was still under construction. My brother and I had paddled down from the top end of Cowichan Lake, looking for a good place for an overnight camp. We couldn't have asked for a nicer landing spot than the protected bay at the Nixon Creek site. The entrance to this campsite is hard to see. Be alert for the side road on the right at km 17.3 (mi 10.7).

The top end of Cowichan Lake is at km 23.2 (mi 14.4) as you reach a major junction. A left turn at the signpost heads into the Nitinat Valley. See **Trip 10** for a description of the drive from Cowichan Lake to the Bamfield cutoff at Franklin Camp and on to Port Alberni. To the right, the road becomes the North Shore Road and continues around the perimeter of Cowichan Lake.

A boat ramp near the head of the lake complements the Fletcher Challenge Heather Campsite. The entrance to this 30 site campground is at the 23.7-km (14.7-mi) mark. It features a beach, nature trails, a covered barbeque pit and sani-station. In the spring and fall, many anglers base camp here and test head-of-the-lake fishing locations. Nixon and Shaw creeks are within range of most boaters. Often at sunset, or right before dawn, large fish lurk in the shallows of Hawes Bay or the waters at the head of the lake.

Keep to the right as you round the west end of Cowichan Lake. Left turns are generally logging spur roads. At km 26.6 (mi 16.5), a side road, to the right, angles down to the remains of the Shaw Creek log dump. All that is left today are pilings and charred timbers of a once important lake access point from the days when lumber was hauled by rail to lakeside booming grounds. Logging opened up the Cowichan Lake district at the turn of the century and remains the primary industry of the area.

Canoeists will find the top end of Cowichan Lake a paddler's paradise. Whether you base at the Heather Campsite or carry wilderness gear and travel to a primitive site along the lakeshore, there is lots to see and do. I particularly like the old trestle on the north side of the lake and the log dump near Shaw Creek. Small coves, accessible only by boat, can be explored — and in some shallow parts of the lake, only a canoe or kayak is practical. You can work your way up Nixon and Shaw creeks a short distance; you then have to line your craft upriver until the shallowing at gravel bars impedes further water progress. From here, you're on foot.

Wave conditions are somewhat less of a problem at the top end of Cowichan Lake after an afternoon of steady westerly winds than in wider lake sections, where whitecapped, rolling trains develop. Paddlers should exercise caution whenever they venture onto lake waters. Any large lake on Vancouver Island should be treated with respect. Know your limitations and

Trolling the creek mouths is one way to fish Cowichan Lake.

be cognizant of weather shifts.

Two more B.C. Forest Service wilderness campsites lie along the North Shore Road: Maple Grove (km 37.9/mi 23.5) and Pine Point (km 39.8/mi 24.7). These sites are open seasonally from mid-May to late September. Over the summer, these campgrounds fill up early. It's a good idea to plan on an early arrival to secure a spot.

The road continues eastward toward Youbou, and curves inland to cross the Cottonwood Creek bridge. At km 43.1 (mi 26.7) you'll reach paved road at the Youbou mill. This is the end of the logging-road portion of our loop around Cowichan Lake.

You can journey from Youbou to Lake Cowichan village on the Youbou Highway or cut off the main road onto Meade Creek Road for more backroads travel. The turnoff is 9 km (5.6 mi) from the mill parking lot. Continue 2 km (1.2 mi) beyond this junction (along the main highway) for the paved road to Teleglobe Canada's Lake Cowichan Earth Station. Free 45-minute guided tours are available to the public from mid-June to Labour Day. A viewing of two 30 m (98 ft) parabolic antennae highlights the tour at this telecommunications facility.

The trailhead for the Diddon-Price hiking trail is right before the Teleglobe Canada installation. This steep path climbs the mountain directly behind the Earth Station and provides hikers with several scenic vantage points looking out over Cowichan Lake. Children will enjoy the lower section

49

with its fairyland of natural wonders.

Meade Creek Road runs south from the Youbou Highway to pass the entrance to the B.C. Forest Service Springs Beach picnic site. A stately stand of timber surrounds this North Arm recreation spot. Marble Bay Road (1.6 km/1 mi from the highway junction) winds in to a small bay of the same name and on to the Boy Scout camp near Bald Mountain. The gate at the camp property line is normally locked. You can make arrangements to use one of the many area hiking trails by phoning Gloria Carnell at (604) 749-3578.

Eventually, Meade Creek Road hooks into North Shore Road. A left turn here heads back to the Youbou Highway, close to the Teleglobe Canada Road. Turn right and drive 2 km (l.2 mi) to Marina Park in Lake Cowichan. There is a boat launch and public dock near the Cowichan Lake weir. From this tiny park it's l km (0.6 mi) to the bridge over the Cowichan River — the start of our lake circle trip.

You can easily complete a loop drive around Cowichan Lake in one day; however, you'll probably want to spend at least a few days at one of the many lakeshore campsites for a longer look at the region's natural beauty.

Contacts:

Fletcher Challenge (Caycuse) (604) 745-3324; B.C. Forest Service (Duncan) (604) 746-5123; Cowichan Lake Research Station (Mesachie Lake) (604) 749-6811; Teleglobe Canada (Lake Cowichan) (604) 749-6646; Ministry of Parks (Victoria) (604) 387-5002; Public Information Officer (604) 387-4609/387-3940.

Maps/Guides:

Renfrew, Cowichan and Nitinat Visitor's Guide, (Fletcher Challenge); *Hiking Trails Vol.II*; *Guide to Forest Land of Southern Vancouver Island*; Topographical Maps: 92C16 *Cowichan Lake* (1:50,000); 92C/NE *Nitinat Lake* (1:125,000).

Nearest Services:

Lake Cowichan; Mesachie Lake; Honeymoon Bay; Youbou.

Trip 10: Backroads: Cowichan Lake to Port Alberni

In Brief:

For a change of pace and scenery, many up-Island travellers choose to take the backroads from Cowichan Lake through the Nitinat Valley to Port Alberni. Forest-company campgrounds, primitive campsites, old trestles and fishing lakes lie along these logging arteries. This is the route paddlers take to the canoeing country around Nitinat Lake; those going to Bamfield and the north end of the West Coast Trail or the trailhead for the giant spruce groves in the Carmanah Valley also follow parts of these roads.

Access:

Drive to the west end of Cowichan Lake (see **Trip 9**) and take the Nitinat/Alberni turn. Route follows gravel mainlines (combined-use roads). Secondary roads may be rough. You may encounter heavy industrial traffic between Nitinat Lake and Franklin Camp.

Description:

The starting point of the backroads run to the top end of Nitinat Lake through to Port Alberni is at the west end of Cowichan Lake. Access to this point is described in the loop around Cowichan Lake in **Trip 9**. From the signposted Nitinat turn, it's about 2 km (1.2 mi) to a road on the right cutting off the mainline. This secondary road goes up the Nitinat River Valley. In 1988, Fletcher Challenge barricaded two bridges in this region after the spans were found to be unsafe for vehicular traffic.

One of the bridges, on the Tuck Lake access road, was blocked with a pile of earth, preventing campers from driving to a riverside campsite on the Nitinat River or on to the tiny camping spot on Tuck Lake shores. The second bridge, farther up the river valley at Redbed Creek was also blocked. This effectively severed the road on which you used to be able to hook into the

Nanaimo Lakes region via a steep switchback near Mount Hooper. You can still explore some of the backroads in this vicinity to reach picturesque riverside hideaways. Determined outdoorsmen will hike in to Tuck Lake for great spring and fall fishing action.

On one trip on these backroads, a friend and I came upon a mink in the middle of the road. As soon as it saw our car round the corner, the animal slinked off into dense underbrush. It's not uncommon to see deer and the occasional black bear in the forests.

There are many disused railway bridges on Island backroads. They harken back to the days when lumber was moved by rail; not the mammoth trucks used by the logging companies today. The weathered trestle at Vernon Creek will intrigue travellers. A few years ago, this relic of early logging was all but obscured by thick, roadside vegetation. Now, however, much of the tree cover has been cleared. An information signpost has been erected at the site giving historical background on the aging span, which was originally constructed in 1933 by Industrial Timber Mills of Youbou.

Road bridges are numerous on the journey through the Nitinat Valley. Some cross boisterous creeks; others span deep ravines and gorges. About 10 km (6 mi) from the west end of Cowichan Lake, the mainline passes one creek where the bridge seemed to wash out every year. If you look closely to your right, you might discern the old roadbed and washout spot, now being reclaimed by the forest. It's easy to see why the washouts occurred, what with the debris and logs piled along the creekside: victims of spring flooding. The new bridge was constructed higher upstream than the old one.

One part of the route becomes a one-way artery for a short stretch. Emphatic signs warn of active logging on many spur roads in the section. These are off-limits for travellers during normal working hours (usually between 6 a.m. and 5 p.m.).

The Nitinat River becomes the focal point of attention as the road follows its banks. MacMillan Bloedel has established a small riverside picnic site along the river. The access to this primitive locale is to the right, just before the 'T' junction near the Nitinat River bridge. Carmanah Main is to the left; Alberni travellers will turn right and cross the Nitinat River bridge. There is a large signpost at this corner. Let's take a short side trip down Carmanah Main to a popular campsite on the shores of Nitinat Lake.

Turn left and drive down Carmanah Main, over the Campus Creek bridge to the 7.8 km (4.8 mi) mark. This is the turn for MacMillan Bloedel/ B.C. Forest Service Nitinat Lake Campsite, on the south side of the lake. There are a limited number of wilderness campsites at this location, and over the summer, it does fill up.

Sailboarders have discovered the campsite and the Nitinat winds that are ideal for windsurfing. By late morning, a steady breeze is usually blowing. That's when the lake waters are crowded with the colourful sails and deft manoeuvrings of the sailboarding set. Their numbers thin out in the afternoon; steady winds and the resultant wave action make water conditions dicey for all but the more experienced at the sport.

I like to base at the Nitinat Campsite in the early season. Then, many of the low-lying spots and shoreline are blanketed with small branches, chunks of wood, errant tree limbs and the occasional larger log. The storms and high waters of winter have left their mark — and a ready supply of wood for campfires.

When the wind is down, Nitinat Lake takes on a tranquil look. Knob Point can be seen on the north side. This is the normal launching point for paddlers venturing into the Nitinat Triangle lake chain (see **Trip 12**). You might see ducks gliding by, bobbing in a gentle swell among marker buoys of submerged crab traps. The barking of seals can sometimes be heard; or the drone of a solitary motorboat breaking the morning stillness.

There are massive trees along the Nitinat shoreline near the campsite. Some have toppled over, leaving huge roots and trunks on the beach. During a sudden shower, I've waited out the downpour in the protection of one of these forest giants. Caycuse Creek pours into Nitinat Lake a short distance from the campsite. There is a trail through the woods leading to the creekmouth or you can walk there along the lakeshore. An old homemade canoe, derelict and piled high with driftwood, once lay above the high-tide line, about halfway down to the creek. Its paint was peeling and the frame rotting from years of neglect and exposure to the elements.

The piped water available at many Island campsites is usually turned off over the winter months. The Nitinat site is no exception. At these times, Caycuse Creek can be a water source. The stream is tidal, so water should be gathered upstream and only at low tide to avoid a saline quality.

In the early spring you should expect heavy shower activity wherever you travel. On Nitinat Lake, you can watch the approach of the recurring rains: a grey-white curtain of moisture and cloud scudding in from the lake's west end. Gumboots will help keep your feet dry. Coupled with adequate foul-weather gear, they'll help you spend more time outdoors, even in spring rains.

You can drive beyond the Nitinat Campsite turn on Carmanah Main to Rosander Main, keeping on the latter to journey to the trailhead for the giant spruce groves in the Carmanah Valley. Updated access information for this region is available from the Sierra Club of B.C. (See **Contacts**).

Turn right at the "T" junction for Bamfield and Port Alberni. The road immediately crosses the Nitinat River bridge. The view from the bridge is worth a look, but don't tarry too long on this narrow span. It's best to park on either end of the bridge and take in the scenery from the riverbank. Once across the river, look for a side road to the right. This goes in to several wilderness campsites: two right on the river; the third providing river access via a short path. Another trail nearby winds in to a deep pool at a bend on the Nitinat River.

The mainline makes a wide curve on the east side of the river and broadens out at the Knob Point cutoff and Nitinat hatchery road, about 2 km (1.2 mi) from the Nitinat River bridge. Paddlers journeying to the Nitinat Triangle lake chain will usually start their adventure from the Knob Point site. (See **Trip 12**.) It's about 9.2 km (5.5 mi) from the turnoff to the launch point. Active logging sometimes restricts public access to Knob Point. Visitors are wise to update current regulations with a quick call to the MacMillan Bloedel Franklin Camp office. (See **Contacts**.)

First-time travellers on the Cowichan/Port Alberni backroads may be surprised to discover pavement starting near the Flora Main junction. This continues (with some gravel stretches) into Franklin Camp and down the Coleman Road to a log dump on Alberni Inlet. Although the hard surface roadway is welcome after the gravel, drivers should be alert for sudden potholes, dips and broken pavement.

You can take Flora Main as an alternate way to Bamfield, if you wish. Active logging and hauling could restrict access on the mainline. To the left of the bridge at the Flora Main turn is an old railway trestle spanning the Little Nitinat River. A number of fishable lakes are along the Flora Main route. (See **Trip 14**.)

You'll pass two lakes on your approach to Franklin Camp: Francis and Darlington lakes. There is a natural boat launch and float on Francis Lake. Some anglers try their luck right off the dock. I've had success trolling along the north shore. On one trip, a friend and I canoed over to the northwest side of Francis Lake and set up camp at a wilderness site there. Francis Lake is larger than Darlington Lake, and both are hemmed in by steep mountains. On the drive along Francis, roadside waterfalls can be seen on the streams that run into the lake. These can be clamorous during periods of heavy rains.

The turn for Bamfield and Pachena Bay, the northern terminus of the West Coast Trail, is at Franklin Camp. Those heading into these areas will cut left at the Bamfield signpost. This jaunt is detailed in **Trip 14**. Keep straight and then right for Port Alberni, following the road markers.

In recent years, heavy hauling has been going on in the Nitinat and Franklin Camp woodlands. Most main roads in this district are classified as combined-use arteries; yet those people who don't fancy journeying along narrow, winding logging roads with the possibility of encountering one of the

An aging trestle still stands near the Flora Main cutoff.

loaded off-road trucks can wait till after weekday working hours before heading out. Some people, myself included, often travel at night. Not all the trucks you might meet will be carrying loads of timber. We crawled up a steep hill near Parson Creek in the wake of an unloaded truck — not only was its tailend hoisted up piggy-back style, but the vehicle was pulling a secondary trailer as well. Some logging trucks have nicknames painted on their cabs. Names like "Log Hog " and "Quick Nick " are two such names we've picked out on our travels.

It's around 4l km (25.5 mi) from Franklin Camp to the outskirts of Port Alberni. Backroaders can explore the Thistle Mine Road giving access to Lizard, Duck, and Father and Son lakes. Further along is the Camp A turn that leads to an Alberni Inlet point.

Some great views of the inlet can be had from the logging road. There are a couple of pulloffs in this area to stop and see the vista with the bustling boat traffic on Alberni Inlet waters. Make sure you park well off the travelled portion of the road. You won't always have good weather and good views, of course. On many trips, I've encountered heavy fogs in this vicinity: mists that obliterate everything around you.

About 30 km (18.6 mi) from Franklin Camp is the entrance to China Creek Park. This campground is jam-packed with visitors over the summer. Most are salt-water anglers who base at the marina/RV campsite and try their luck in inlet waters. Some even venture as far as Barkley Sound. The camping at this facility is right on the inlet and boat rentals are available.

As you near Port Alberni, you'll drive by the Cameron Division work yards. Turn left at the signpost for Port Alberni. Pavement is reached at the intersection with Ships Creek Road, about 11 km (6.8 mi) from the China Creek Park road. Backroaders can continue straight ahead at the Cameron Division yards to Bainbridge Lake. This lake is classified as a seniors- and kids-only lake. The road runs into the Cameron River Valley and the Mount Arrowsmith area.

The drive to Port Alberni from Cowichan Lake offers the visitor the choice of many Island destinations along usually well- maintained backroads. Utilizing the proper degree of caution when journeying on these logging-road networks, outdoorsmen can enjoy a scenic alternate route to many up-Island locales.

Contacts:

Fletcher Challenge (Caycuse) (604) 745-3324; MacMillan Bloedel (Franklin Camp) (604) 723-9471; MacMillan Bloedel (Cameron Division) (604) 723-3585; Sierra Club of B.C. (Victoria) (604) 386-5255; B.C. Forest Service (Port Alberni) (604) 724-9205.

Maps/Guides:

Renfrew, Cowichan and Nitinat Visitor's Guide, (Fletcher Challenge); *Recreation and Logging Road Guide to Tree Farm Licence • 44* (east map), (MacMillan Bloedel); *Carmanah Valley-Road Access and Hiking Trail Guide*,(Western Canada Wilderness Committee); *Guide to Forest Land of Southern Vancouver Island*; Topographical Maps: 92C16 *Cowichan Lake* (1:50,000); 92C15 *Little Nitinat River* (1:50,000); 92F2 *Alberni Inlet* (1:50,000); 92F/SE *Port Alberni* (1:125,000); 92C/NE *Nitinat Lake* (1:125,000).

Nearest Services:

Lake Cowichan Region; Port Alberni.

Trip 11: Canoeing Nitinat Lake

In Brief:

Big-lake paddling enthusiasts can choose from a number of large lakes on Vancouver Island. But perhaps the most challenging one of all is Nitinat Lake. Connected to the Pacific Ocean by the infamous Nitinat Narrows, the lake is susceptible to daily tidal fluctuations and strong winds. Nitinat is usually windswept by midday and its steep shorelines contribute to dangerous chop and confused sea conditions. By travelling in the early morning, ahead of the daily winds, or during one of Nitinat's calmer moods, you can journey to secluded beaches and down to the narrows. Brown's Bay Trail, a primitive path, runs from a bay (of the same name) east of the narrows to Clo-oose. Caution, though, is a keyword on Nitinat Lake — a prime setting for a true wilderness experience.

Access:

Launch Points:

Mac/Blo-B.C. Forest Service Campsite: turn left at the Nitinat River bridge (see **Trip 10**) and drive 7.8 km (4.6 mi) to the campsite turn).

Knob Point: from the Cowichan/Port Alberni mainline along the northwest side of Nitinat Lake take the Knob Point access road (hatchery turn) 2 km (1.2 mi) beyond the Nitinat River bridge. (See **Trip 10**.)

Description:

The Nitinat region on Lower Vancouver Island is a canoeist's paradise and the setting for overnight trips or more extended wilderness excursions by many paddlers. Along the north shore of Nitinat Lake is the access to the Nitinat Triangle: a lake chain that includes Squalicum, Hobiton, Tsusiat and Tsuquadra lakes. Travelling down to the Nitinat Narrows will bring visitors to a point midway along the West Coast Trail, and requires voyaging down almost the full length of Nitinat Lake. It's a challenging undertaking.

Nitinat Lake is a unique body of water in that it is the only tidal lake on the Island. Technically it should be called Nitinat Inlet, affected as it is by the infamous narrows at its western end. The lake is fed by numerous watersheds: notably the Nitinat, Caycuse and Hobiton river systems. The upper end is of a saline quality. Winds are usually up by late morning on Nitinat Lake, making the going tough in a canoe or kayak; if it's really blowing, no small craft will be out bucking the waves.

The most striking feature noticed about the lake is the sea influence. Jellyfish abound at certain times, starfish and anemones cling precariously to the rocky cliffs and sunken shoreline boulders beneath lake waters and the smell of the ocean is unmistakable.

There are two primary access points on Nitinat Lake: the MacMillan Bloedel/B.C. Forest Service Campsite on the south shore and the Fletcher Challenge Knob Point site on the north side. The latter is the jumping-off spot for adventurers heading into the Nitinat Triangle. (See **Trip 12**.)

An all-hours access logging mainline leads to Nitinat Lake via Cowichan Lake. You can also travel roads down from Port Alberni to reach the lakehead. (See **Trip 10**.) Working hours are normally 6 a.m. to 5 p.m. for the loggers on weekdays, so be wary of logging trucks and heavy industrial traffic at these times. Traffic can be noticeably heavy around the top end of Nitinat Lake through to Franklin Camp.

Logging is quite evident on the mountainsides visible from Nitinat Lake as the cutters chew their way to the coast. Environmentalists continue to lobby for wider boundaries between coastal logging and the West Coast Trail. Carmanah Valley's unique grove of giant spruce trees may have a clouded future should the current logging plans for the valley move forward.

The topography of the Nitinat area varies as you travel up and down the lake. In some places, cliffs rise perpendicularly out of the water leaving no possible landing spots. (A bad place to be if you really had to beach.) When the winds arise, these are hazardous paddling grounds due to the bathtub effect of the waves as they rebound off sheer rock faces, creating chop. The land is generally flatter around the creek and rivermouths, and levels out substantially as you near the narrows.

There are a number of Indian reserves scattered along the Nitinat. Respect for these areas should always be maintained. Not all of these are inhabited year-round. Some are used only during the seasonal runs of spawning salmon; a few are indicated by a small shack at a creekmouth or a clearing in the forest.

In the early morning, ahead of the daily winds and waves, it can be easy going on the Nitinat as you pass jutting cliff faces and skim into quiet

Morning mists cloak the waters of Nitinat Lake.

bays. On one trip, my paddling partner and I startled a heron, which then wheeled up from its perch — its head hunched like an ancient pterodactyl — and slowly beat its way to the solitude of an adjoining cove. It's not uncommon to see eagles and hawks soaring high above the mountains and valleys. To walk along a rocky beach and come upon an eagle gorging itself on the flesh of a freshly-caught salmon; to see this magnificient bird spread its wings in flight, giving a cry of rage at having to delay its dinner, is a sight never to be forgotten.

Water birds of many types are found on the Nitinat, incuding mergansers, loons and others. Keep an eye out for otters and seals, especially towards the narrows. The seals have a habit of lifting their heads out of the water and curiously peering around before suddenly diving below the surface. They often startle paddlers.

A third of the way down to the narrows, a long, slender waterfall, known as Sitting Lady Falls, tumbles down the steep terrain west of Mount Rosander. On one 1977 journey, our party stopped at the falls to replenish our water supply and take a break. The unpredictable bathtub chop of the lake waters forced us to secure the canoe safely above the reach of the lake waves. We followed the natural contours of the rocks and carefully ascended the lower part of the falls. We took care not to slip on wet rocks or moss. The tumbling waters of the cascade had gouged a series of natural pools in the rugged shoreface. Nothing felt better after a sweltering afternoon's paddle than a refreshing dip in one of the chill-water tubs: complete with running water and a spectacular view to the west.

It cannot be over-emphasized that Nitinat Lake should be treated with respect. You don't want to be caught in rough seas in areas where safe landings are impossible. The lake has many twists and turns and the daily winds come up early to produce heavy swell. Early morning is the best time for lake travel, yet on some days, even then you might be forced to wait out the gusts and hole up until calmer conditions prevail.

Daykins Bay is to the south of the falls. A logging camp used to be situated on the shore here. A small islet offshore makes a good choice for a rest stop. In the waters adjacent to Nitinat Cone, the wind can challenge paddlers as they will be moving due west. If the going gets tricky, there are some quieter bays in this vicinity in which to drift.

Nitinat Lake constricts as you near Brown's Bay, and begins a serpentine curve to the narrows. Behind a structure hidden in the trees at **Brown's Bay**, a primitive trail can be found that leads in to Clo-oose, on the coast. While relatively short in length, (under 3 km/2 mi), this path can be arduous. The trail is unimproved and requires hikers to traverse slick, moss-covered logs and dilapidated bridges. It can be extremely muddy, especially near Clo- oose Lake, about halfway along.

Some paddlers will canoe down Nitinat Lake to Brown's Bay, where they will then hike in to the West Coast Trail along the Brown's Bay Trail. This trail offers a test of hiking skills and dexterity for the many hikers desiring that type of experience. Beyond Brown's Bay, heading to the narrows, the tidal currents will be more evident — when they are really flowing, they can be treacherous, even for experienced paddlers.

Whyac, the old Indian village at the narrows, is one of the earliest settlements on the west coast. A ghostly tranquility rests over the site now, sitting high on a rocky headland overlooking the vast Pacific swell. Near Whyac, you can observe powerful ocean tides as they fluctuate through the constricted waterway entering Nitinat Lake. West Coast Trail hikers are ferried across the narrows by residents of the reserve at the head of Nitinat Lake. The Indians also maintain isolated cabins at various spots along the lake.

Whenever I tackle the narrows in a canoe, it's just prior to slack water on an ebb tide. At slack tide (a period of only 5 or 6 minutes) the current is minimal, although the sea swell still affects conditions in the narrows. Only once (out of five attempts) have water conditions been favourable for a canoeing partner and me to continue beyond Whyac to Tsuquanah Point. Even then we didn't tarry long — as the tide turned to flood and the current increased, we left the breaker-lashed open coastline and slowly drifted back towards the main part of Nitinat Lake.

The Nitinat was once the scene of a thriving salmon industry. The Lummi Bay cannery was built in 1921 near Whyac. You can still see the ruins of this facility. A fish camp was once located at Brown's Bay. Nets were strung across the narrows, almost depleting the run. It has never been the same since. Without the supply of fish, the cannery closed down.

In the 1930s, one logging company, who operated at the upper end of Nitinat Lake, blasted away some rocks just inside the narrows. This was done to facilitate the manoeuvre of boomed logs that were towed through the passage. While this helped the loggers, it became harder from smaller craft to negotiate the entrance to Nitinat Lake. No longer could boaters use the points of rock as they zig-zagged their way against the tidal flow of the narrows.

The *Canadian Tide and Current Tables Vol. 6* indicate times of slack water at Nitinat Narrows (with calculations based on Tofino); however, the area's navigability will vary depending on weather and wave action out in the open sea. You might hear the sound of the whistle buoy offshore near Clo-oose at the narrows. It's easy to mistake its drone for a fog horn — until you hear it on a perfectly clear day. Rain or fog; fair or bright: if the waves and breakers are up, the buoy will be activated, sending its bellow out to passing boats.

When the fishing fleet is active, they sometimes anchor overnight in the small bay near Clo-oose. Sports fishermen are familiar with the narrows. They have to be to ensure safe passage through the waterway and out across the shallow Nitinat Bar, just outside Nitinat Narrows.

We were observing the tidal flow through the narrows once when a young family — father, mother and young daughter — were seen fighting their way in a canoe towards Whyac against a strong flood tide. With great difficulty their small craft was propelled to the quieter cove below Whyac's primitive shacks. For an instant, it appeared as if we were going to be forced into action as a sudden swell toyed with the direction of their canoe just as the family rounded a point of submerged rocks. Luckily, they reached safe shores.

A dangerous loop tour through the narrows and along the open coastline to Tsusiat Falls, and then via Tsusiat and Hobiton lakes back to Nitinat Lake has been completed by some canoeists and kayakers. Weather and tidal conditions at the narrows have to be just right for the passage through constricted Canoe Pass, west of Whyac. There are so many variables, that it's rarely suitable for such an endeavour.

The only thing predictable about weather on the Island's west coast is its unpredictability. Once, we ran into a fog bank crawling in from the Pacific: cold, thick and heavy. The mist obliterated everything around, engulfing us in a chilling shroud. Travel on the lake at such times can be treacherous (a compass may be required), and as you approach the narrows, it's best to allow the fog to burn off a little before continuing your travels.

There are obvious potential dangers for those paddling on Nitinat waters. The wind and waves are two factors. The shallow Nitinat Bar at the lake's mouth causes standing waves and pounding surf at times; there are perilous whirlpools and upwellings in and around Whyac during peak tidal flows — currents that can attain eight knots. The duration of slack water at the narrows is brief and does not coincide with high or low tide. That's why the tidebook is indispensable in making the calculation.

We sometimes read news stories about the loss of life due to carelessness and uncalled-for errors in judgment by Nitinat paddlers. There is no margin for error when canoeing in the vicinity of Whyac. Yet with common sense, some local knowledge, and a healthy respect for the sea, a trip down Nitinat Lake to the narrows can be a rewarding wilderness adventure.

Contacts:

MacMillan Bloedel (Franklin Camp) (604) 723-9471; B.C. Forest Service (Port Alberni) (604) 724-9205.

Maps/Guides:

The West Coast Trail and Nitinat Lakes, (Sierra Club of B.C.); *Pacific Rim Explorer*, (Bruce Obee/Whitecap); *Recreation and Logging Road Guide to Tree Farm Licence No. 44* (east map), (MacMillan Bloedel); *Renfrew, Cowichan and Nitinat Visitor's Guide*, (Fletcher Challenge); *Guide to Forest Land of Southern Vancouver Island*; *Canadian Tide and Current Tables Vol. 6* (Canadian Hydrographic Service); Topographical Maps: Regional Map No. 2 *Parksville/Tofino* (1:125,000); 92C15 *Little Nitinat River* (1:50,000); 92C10 *Carmanah Creek* (1:50,000); 92C/NE *Nitinat Lake* (1:125,000).

Nearest Services:

Lake Cowichan Area; Port Alberni.

Trip 12: The Nitinat Triangle

In Brief:

Paddlers who enjoy a challenging wilderness excursion will want to consider a journey into the Nitinat Triangle, a series of lakes (including Nitinat, Hobiton, Squalicum and Tsusiat) connected by rugged portage trails. There is good fishing in the fresh-water lakes and it is possible to hike a rough trail west of Tsusiat Lake down to the West Coast Trail and Tsusiat Falls.

Access:

Launch Point:

Knob Point: On the northwest side of Nitinat Lake cut off the Cowichan/Alberni mainline at the Knob Point access road (hatchery turn). (See **Trip 10.**) This is a gravel road; may be restricted access.

Description:

One of the better known canoeing regions on Vancouver Island is the Nitinat Triangle, made up of Hobiton, Squalicum and Tsusiat lakes among others. These lakes are located northwest of Nitinat Lake and are connected by portage trails and primitive paths. Travellers should be prepared for some tough going on the somewhat rugged portage routes. By journeying down to Tsusiat Lake, you can then follow a trail leading west to the West Coast Trail and Tsusiat Falls. The launching point for the lake chain is on the northwest shore of tidal Nitinat Lake, at the Fletcher Challenge Knob Point site. There is a steep natural boat ramp here on the forested point.

Nitinat Lake must be paddled from Knob Point down to the mouth of Hobiton Creek. Travellers should note that Nitinat Lake is susceptible to daily winds that spring up by late morning and continue to blow all day. These winds can create heavy swell and whitecaps that can be dangerous paddling waters. Getting an early start will usually avoid the rougher water.

The fishing at Hobiton Lake can be good.

At the mouth of Hobiton Creek there is an Indian reserve. Visitors are expected to respect this area. No camping is allowed without prior permission from the Nitinaht Band.

There are two ways into Hobiton Lake. You can line up the creek or take the portage trail. At certain times of the year, lining up Hobiton Creek is not feasible. The flow may be too high or too low. The lower reaches are rockier and normally the hardest to negotiate. Be prepared to get your feet and legs wet while you line your way upstream. Further along, some deep pools require you to paddle across. The creek is closed to travellers when salmon run up the stream in the fall. The Nitinaht Band maintains a salmon fishery here at that time. Then paddlers have no option but to use the portage trail.

The portage is indicated by a red marker on a point of rock, just south of the Indian reserve boundary. It begins in a small bay beyond the triangular marker. While volunteers periodically clear the path, the portage is still in rough shape. There are muddy sections and windfall to contend with. It's best to make two trips: one with your canoe or kayak; the second carrying your gear.

Wilderness campsites can be found along the north shore of Hobiton Lake. Nearby creeks provide one water source. Some of the more well-known sites are Dead Alder, Hitchie Creek and Cedar Log campsites. As more and more people become aware of the recreation potential of the Nitinat Triangle, the region will reflect the impact of a greater influx of wilderness seekers. During peak periods (June, July and August) firewood can become scarce at the more frequented campsites. It's a good idea to carry and use a portable campstove on your trip.

A rough trail can be hiked in to Squalicum Lake. It's a tough climb and not recommended with a canoe. The trail's start is located about halfway down the south shore of Hobiton. Look for bright ribbons on the trees near a gravel beach area.

Tangled lines are a part of fishing.

Hobiton Lake is dominated by the Hobiton Ridge, which rises sharply on its north side. The Hobiton area is known for its stands of old-growth timber. The lake is ideal for swimming and has good fishing. Everything from bait and bobber to spinning gear will take trout from lake waters. Hotspots tend to be the mouths of creeks flowing down from Hobiton Ridge.

For many adventurers, the portage into Hobiton Lake and back is enough. They are content to spend a few days enjoying the atmosphere of Hobiton. There's something magical about Hobiton Lake, especially on those early mornings when the mist hovers just above the lake water, obliterating everything else. Slowly, it dissipates, melting into gossamer whisps with the rising sun, to be blown away by morning breezes. More adventurous travellers will opt for the second portage — the one from Hobiton over to Tsusiat Lake. It begins on the south side of Hobiton Lake, almost at its southwest end. It too is marked and can be identified near a large log that descends into the lake waters. This trail throws deadfall, mudholes and steep, slick slopes at hikers and those bringing in their canoes. There's a swampy area about halfway along. This region was slowly being destroyed by portagers as they tramped through. Volunteers have since constructed a bypass route to protect fragile vegetation.

Another problem that is becoming more and more evident in the Nitinat Triangle and similar wilderness regions of Vancouver Island is the lack of camping etiquette. Too many people are leaving garbage behind at their campsites. A big culprit is the freeze-dried food packet preferred by backpackers. Even if these are buried, they could soon be dug up by varmints or birds and thus become eyesores to future visitors. The adage "if you pack it in, pack it out" may be over-used; yet it is still under-practised by many.

Tsusiat Lake may be paddled to a log jam near the outlet creek. Campsites along Tsusiat are few and far between, with the best sites on the north shore. One of the better spots is near the southwest-end log jam. You may decide to explore a lagoon on the west side of Tsusiat Lake. From a distance, the entrance is hard to pick out, camouflaged by the topography. It was to this lagoon that the Nitinaht Indians would send their women and children when their territory was under siege from warring enemy tribes.

A trail starts at the log jam at the west end of Tsusiat Lake that can be taken by those keen to reach the West Coast Trail near Tsusiat Falls. This cascade is one of the scenic highlights of the coast trail. I've been along the south trail from Tsusiat, which I understand is in better shape than the one on the north side. As it was, there were some tricky log crossings, slippery deadfall to skirt and thick underbrush to contend with. Some intrepid voyageurs portage their canoes over this rough route to launch into the surf and enter Nitinat Lake via the Nitinat Narrows. With the effort required for such an undertaking, coupled with the extreme danger of open-sea travel and the passage through the narrows, I question the wisdom of the journey. (See **Trip 11**.) It makes more sense to return the way you came in — portages and all.

Contacts:

Superintendent — Pacific Rim National Park (Ucluelet) (604) 726-7721/726-4212; MacMillan Bloedel (Franklin Camp) (604) 723-9471.

Maps/Guides:

The West Coast Trail and Nitinat Lakes (Sierra Club of B.C.); *Pacific Rim Explorer*, (Bruce Obee/Whitecap); *Recreation and Logging Road Guide to Tree Farm Licence No. 44* (east map),(MacMillan Bloedel); *Renfrew, Cowichan and Nitinat Visitors Guide*, (Fletcher Challenge); *Guide to Forest Land of Southern Vancouver Island*; Topographical Maps: Regional Map No. 2 *Parksville/Tofino* (1:125,000); 92C15 *Little Nitinat River* (1:50,000); 92C10 *Carmanah Creek* (1:50,000); 92C/NE *Nitinat Lake* (1:125,000).

Nearest Services:

Lake Cowichan Area; Port Alberni; Bamfield.

Trip 13: The West Coast Trail

In Brief:

Originally established in the early 1900s as a life-saving trail along the stretch of coastline known as the "Graveyard of the Pacific," the West Coast Trail is now part of Pacific Rim National Park. No longer a primitive path, the trail has been improved over the years with cable-car and bridge river crossings, boardwalks and regular trail clearing. It's still a rugged wilderness hike and should not by taken lightly. It's a spectacular 75 km (46.6 mi) trek along west coast beaches, and challenges the body and the mind.

Access:

To Bamfield trailhead: follow logging mainlines from Cowichan Lake to Franklin Camp. (See **Trip 10.**) Take the Bamfield Road from Franklin Camp to Pachena Bay. (See **Trip 14.**)

Port Renfrew trailhead: take Highway 14 (West Coast Road) to Port Renfrew. (See **Trip 1.**) Follow signs to ferry crossing at Gordon River.

Via Nitinat Lake: experienced paddlers can journey down Nitinat Lake to reach the West Coast Trail via the unimproved Brown's Bay Trail or at Nitinat Narrows. (See **Trip 11.**)

Description:

The West Coast Trail snakes along the wild coastline of Vancouver Island from Pachena Bay (near Bamfield) south to Port Renfrew. Once a life-saving trail to aid in the rescue of shipwrecked mariners, it is now part of Pacific Rim National Park. The 75 km (46.6 mi) trail has been upgraded over the years. River crossings are now easier since the construction of bridges and cable cars. Boardwalks skirt wet terrain and the trail is regularly cleared of brush.

It takes about a week to walk the complete length of the trail at a reasonable pace. Hikers should be well-equipped for the wilderness; there are

Many West Coast Trail hikers take the M.V. Lady Rose *out of Port Alberni.*

no services along the way. Even in the summer, chilling fogs are common on the coast. Hypothermia is one of the greatest dangers for hikers and should be guarded against. A government pamphlet about the West Coast Trail, complete with topographical maps, hints and points of interest is available at Maps B.C. in Victoria, the Sierra Club's Victoria office, and some sporting goods stores. It's well suited for conditions on the trail as it's printed on waterproof paper.

Some visitors have neither the time nor the inclination to hike the complete trail. They will opt for a partial trip, often from Bamfield to Michigan Creek; or farther afield to Tsusiat Falls, a trail highlight. There are two ferry crossings: at Nitinat Narrows about halfway along the coast and at Gordon River. There is a small fee levied for these crossings.

You can begin your trek either in Port Renfrew or Bamfield. The northern section is considered the easiest; the southern half is more challenging. For that reason, many people planning on doing the complete trail, will start at the Bamfield trailhead. By the time you hit the tougher stretches, packs will be lighter and you'll be conditioned by a few days hiking. The choice of starting points is up to you.

There is a Parks Branch registration and information booth located at Pachena Bay, the northern terminus of the West Coast Trail. The beach at Pachena is a beautiful strand of sand — a great introduction to area scenery.

Between Pachena Bay and Pachena Point lighthouse there is a lot of up-and-down hiking required. A long wooden bridge spans a gulley near the trailhead. A friend and I passed through here when the bridge was still under construction. We had to descend the muddy banks and climb slick slopes on the far side of the small ravine. The bridge certainly makes this section of the path a lot easier to negotiate. You'll follow what is really an old road to the lighthouse, so the trail is wide here. Rough paths angle off the main trail to several water-access points. It can be difficult to hike these routes as most are unimproved.

One of the more spectacular viewpoints is known as the Flat Rocks lookout. In the spring and fall, sea lions can be seen sunning themselves on the rocks. Take care here, the drop is sheer. The Pachena lighthouse is a good subject for photographs. From here the trail climbs a bit before dropping down to Michigan Creek and the first of many beach-camping locales.

At low tide, the shelf is exposed revealing reefs and tidepools. A friend of mine was exploring the reef when he discovered the tide must have shifted. He was able to return to shore without wetting his feet, but he did almost get trapped out on the rocks. Hikers should take care when walking in low tide zones. The boiler from the *Michigan*, a ship that went down in 1893, is visible on the rocks near Michigan Creek. Remnants from other shipwrecks are found all along the West Coast Trail. This part of the west coast was called the Graveyard of the Pacific — and with good reason.

A bridge crosses Michigan Creek. At tides below 3.6 m (12 ft) you can follow the beach from this point to Tsocowis Creek. The Darling River is between these streams and is another good region for camping. A cable car carries travellers over the river. If water flow is low enough, nimble hikers can pick their way over on creekbed stones. A cave along the beach to the east is worth a look. At Tsocowis Creek, you must take the trail around an impassable headland. A bridge along this stretch spans Billy Goat Creek. You'll pass an abandoned donkey engine, a relic from the turn of the last century when the original life-saving trail was built. Also along this part of the trail is a viewpoint looking down on the scene of the grounding of the *Valencia*, in 1906. One hundred and twenty-six lives were lost.

You can take the next beach access and keep along the shore to the Klanawa River if the tides are below 3.6 m (12 ft). Parts of this beach are rocky and dotted with large, slippery boulders that are tricky to walk on. Coastal travellers will encounter many such shorelines. Other beaches are of fine sand, and unless you walk on harder-packed ground, carrying a heavy pack can be tedious in these areas.

Another cable car is situated at the Klanawa River. This waterway is relatively wide, with a rocky dropoff into the ocean. A primitive cabin sits on the east side of the river. We once arrived at the Klanawa when a series of squalls were passing through. The cold seeped into our bodies as we stopped. A driftwood fire, hastily set up, soon warded off the chill. An area at the mouth of the Klanawa River provides another good camping locale, but be careful to set up your tent well above the tidal section of the river. Some campers have received a surprise at night and discovered they've been soaked by high-tide waters backing up the Klanawa.

An impeding headland forces hikers once again to take the trail between the Klanawa River and Tsusiat Point. This part of the path runs high above the ocean. On the east side of the Tsusiat River bridge, look for the beach access that descends sharply to the sea via a long series of wooden steps. The camping spot near the base of Tsusiat Falls is the most popular tenting ground on the West Coast Trail. The 18.3 m (60 ft) cascade is often used as a navigational aid by boaters out on the Pacific.

The route down to the falls is steep with many wooden ladders on the way. It's definitely worth the effort. Unfortunately, firewood becomes scarce at the falls due to the hundreds of campers who throng to the area over the summer. If you're seeking solitude, that's one thing you won't find at Tsusiat Falls; unless you're travelling during the off-season, as more people are now doing. Two rugged trails follow either side of the Tsusiat River up to Tsusiat Lake. There is much deadfall to climb over and sections of the paths are muddy. This is a connecting link to Nitinat Triangle canoeing country. (See **Trip 12**.)

Tsusiat Point features the famous landmark called Hole-in the Wall, a sea-carved archway in the rocks. Near Tsuquadra Point, there are sea caves which can be investigated at low tide. Respect this area — it is part of an Indian reserve. Tsuquadra Point must be skirted via trails due to the impassable headland there. Tsusiat Point is passable when tides are low enough. There is a nice beach between Tsuquadra Point and Nitinat Narrows. Here, jagged pinnacles of rock rise up from the sands to break the smooth contours of this sloping strand. At the east end of this beach the trail can be rejoined. It winds through lush salal to the narrows. Hikers must be ferried across this tidal waterway at the outlet to Nitinat Lake by local Indians. A nominal fee is charged for this service.

You can journey down the length of Nitinat Lake to the narrows, as friends and I have done a number of times. Currents in the narrows are treacherous and changeable. Nitinat Lake tends to become windswept by mid-morning, so extreme caution must be exercised on such an outing. (See **Trip 11**.)

Several tales gleaned from the Indians tell of numerous times when impatient hikers have borrowed boats belonging to the reserve to cross the turbulent narrows. More often than not, these boats were improperly beached,

Island trails test a hiker's concentration and patience.

only to be washed away with the next high tide. From mid-May to the end of September (peak periods for trail hiking) someone is usually around to provide ferry service. If you do have to wait a bit, it's not for very long.

In 1979, my brother and I encountered two fellow outdoorsmen who had been stranded on the west side of the narrows. Their canoe had been thoughtlessly borrowed by other hikers. We had canoed to Whyac and were on the east shore viewing the tidal flow when we first saw the pair. We waited for slack water and towed their craft over to them.

The trail runs behind the old Indian village of Whyac to Clo-oose, a former west coast settlement. The Brown's Bay Trail cuts into a bay of the same name on Nitinat Lake. This trail, starting near Clo-oose, is unimproved and quite challenging. It is sometimes used as a link to the West Coast Trail by those paddling down Nitinat Lake. (See **Trip 11**.)

Boardwalks have been built between the narrows and the Cheewhat River. A suspension bridge crosses this river. When translated, *Cheewhat* means "river of urine" due to its yellow colour. The water comes from boggy regions upstream and originates at Cheewhat Lake. From the Cheewhat all the way to Owen Point, difficult surge channels confront beach hikers. It is imperative that travellers be up-to-date on tidal information. This data is

71

found in the *Canadian Tide and Current Tables: Vol. 6*. The listings tabulated for Tofino are the ones to use. It should be noted that all tidal information is based on the assumption of calm seas. Winds and storms can cause a rise in tides: an occurrence that could trap unwary hikers out on the shelf. Hikers should respect the sea and take no unnecessary chances when venturing in potentially dangerous areas.

One surge channel is located just east of Dare Point. Beach-access trails will bring you up to the main path on which you can bypass this potential problem spot during adverse tide conditions. Just offshore from the Carmanah Point lighthouse is another seasonal sea lion sunning ground. Most hikers take the land route over the headland at Carmanah Point to avoid scrambling over slippery rocks on the beach.

East of Carmanah Point down to Vancouver Point hikers must follow the shoreline route. If tides are low enough, you can keep to the beach, to cross Walbran Creek on a cable car and then continue on to Logan Creek. There are some problem areas to note. Many hikers opt for the inland-trail route between these points.

You have to take into account that during rainy periods, many streams along the West Coast Trail will enter a flood stage. Often access to the land trail is directly up the creeks. If their flow is too high, travel will be impossible in the vicinity of the creekmouths. Hikers should note prevailing weather patterns and temper their choice of routes accordingly.

Perhaps the most dangerous place on the West Coast Trail is the surge channel at Adrenaline Creek. The sea chasm extends all the way to a shoreline cliff. It is here that travellers must inch along a narrow ledge when tides are below 1.7 m (5.5 ft) and the weather is dry. You can use an exposed rock in the middle of the channel to help in this risky passage. But that's not all. Even with the proper low tide and calm seas, the rocks here remain wet due to a waterfall at this same locale. Inexperienced hikers should avoid this area. Even trail veterans prefer the inland trail to taking a chance along the dangerous beach route. An additional deterrent is the fact that once by the surge channel, you must rejoin the land trail at Logan Creek to get to Cullite Cove and over to Sandstone Creek — and that involves wading Logan Creek. This is practical only when Logan's flow is low.

Between Logan Creek and Sandstone Creek, two impeding headlands force hikers inland through some swampy terrain. Boardwalks in this area now make it easier to traverse the bog. In years previous to park improvements, hikers had to slog through the quagmire in often thigh-deep mud.

It is possible to travel along the sandstone shelf from Sandstone Creek to Camper Bay (when the tides are right), but it is difficult and not recommended for those venturing east towards Port Renfrew. It's not much easier for those travelling from east to west. You have to climb along Sandstone Creek to rejoin the trail; and only when this stream's flow is minimal. At the proper low tide, this route requires climbing down from the shelf and wading a section of ocean to Sandstone Creek. Once up the mud-slick streambed, you then have to scale a waterfall with the help of a cable. Struggling down Sandstone Creek and climbing up onto the shelf is extremely hard and potentially dangerous, hence the suggestions in most guidebooks and park literature NOT to attempt this passage when journeying west to east.

There is an excellent campsite at Camper Bay, but it does become crowded over the summer. From this point, take the inland trail east of Trisle Creek to avoid yet another headland. This part of the path cuts through a major blowdown. In this area, trees lie toppled over on top of one another as a result of severe winds.

If you're determined to keep to the beach as much as possible, you can take the next beach access onto the shelf and work your way around Owen Point all the way to Thrasher Cove. There are some tricky surge channels to get around, and many beach areas are strewn with slippery boulders. It's easy to become trapped in some regions by incoming tides, so make sure your tidal calculations are correct.

The Ministry of Parks trail map suggests you not travel eastward on the shelf between the first beach access trail after Camper Bay and the problematic surge channel halfway to the next rough path up to the land route. It's also noted that the going is easier from Owen Point to Thrasher Cove than hiking the beach from the opposite direction. A ferry service is available to take hikers to and from the Gordon River trailhead and Thrasher Cove.

It's about 1 km (0.6 mi) from Thrasher Cove up to the main trail. A series of steep ladders must be negotiated on the climb up or down to this location. From the Thrasher Cove cutoff to the Gordon River crossing, the trail slithers through the second growth forest. There is a fair amount of up and down travel and the usual muddy sections as well as log crossings over tiny creeks and gulleys. Viewpoints looking over Port San Juan and out to the Olympic Mountains in Washington state break the constant walking through the woods. One break in the trees is near the highest point on the West Coast Trail. Another point of interest is the old donkey engine from an earlier era of logging. The trail ends (or begins) at the Gordon River.

The West Coast Trail should not be taken lightly, even with the many improvements now in place. Visitors should go equipped for the wilderness and prepared for the unexpected. Respect for the sea and a precise knowledge of tides is essential. Hiking all or part of the trail establishes a deep understanding of one's own limitations; you learn to interact with the environment around you; and you certainly experience a feeling of accomplishment when the hike is over. The real challenge is not the trail itself, but how you react to the many variables encountered along the rugged route.

Contacts:

Ministry of Parks (Victoria) (604) 387-5002; Public Information Officer (604) 387-4609/387-3940; Superintendent-Pacific Rim National Park (Ucluelet) (604) 726-7721/726-4212; Gordon River ferry service (Port Renfrew) Norm Smith-(604) 647-5430.

Maps/Guides:

West Coast Trail water resistant map published by the Ministry of Parks; *The West Coast Trail and Nitinat Lakes*, (the Sierra Club of B.C.); *Pacific Rim Explorer*, (Obee/Whitecap); *Guide to Forest Land of Southern Vancouver Island*; *Canadian Tide and Current Tables Vol. 6*, (Canadian Hydrographic Service); Topographical Maps: 92C9 *Port Renfrew* (1:50,000); 92C10 *Carmanah Creek* (1:50,000); 92C14 *Barkley Sound* (1:50,000); Regional Map No. 2 *Parksville/Tofino* (1:125,000); 92C/NE *Nitinat Lake* (1:125,000).

Nearest Services:

Bamfield; Port Renfrew.

Trip 14: Backroads To Bamfield

In Brief:

Should you be travelling to Bamfield, possibly to tackle the West Coast Trail, you might consider spending some time exploring the sites on the way there. Sarita, Pachena and Frederick lakes are known to fresh-water fishermen; Poett Nook marina and RV park caters to Barkley Sound salt-water anglers. Countless backroads intersect the Bamfield Road, leading visitors to secluded backwoods locales. You can even loop tour by taking the Bamfield Road in and Flora Main on your way out.

Access:

Take the Bamfield Road turn at Franklin Camp on the Cowichan/ Alberni backroads. (See **Trip 10.**) Route is a gravel mainline (Combined-use road). Secondary roads may be rough; could require four-by-four. Some areas may be restricted access.

Description:

Backwoods browsers will often encounter secondary roads on jaunts down logging mainlines. Exploring some of them can lead to clandestine camping locations, secret fishing spots and the remains of old logging camps and work sites. Not all the roads are marked on every map; some aren't on any maps. If you're at all curious on your outings, you'll just have to scout out the unmarked routes by trial and error.

On many of my Island forays, I've come upon areas still harbouring disused logging machinery. Old camp structures, some standing, others flattened over time, harken back to days gone by. Disused trestles that once shuddered with the passage of lumber carried by rail, cross deep ravines.

Rough side roads, many requiring hiking, lead in to lakes, rivers and streams. All you have to do is investigate the intriguing byways to discover your own secret nook in Island woodlands. A short climb up a spur road often leads to a superb vista or seascape just begging to be captured on film. The less-travelled backroads are often wandered by black bears and other wildlife.

An area on the Lower Island with much to see and do both on the mainlines and along more overgrown routes is the Bamfield region. There are many fresh-water lakes for trout fishing and canoeing, and plenty of backroads to explore.

We'll start at Franklin Camp, along the Cowichan/Alberni backroad network. (See **Trip 10.**) The road is classified as a combined- use artery. It can be a dusty drive in the summer with lots of pulling over if there is industrial traffic using the road. You may encounter crummies (small buses which carry loggers to and from work sites), heavy duty company pickups and logging trucks — loaded and unloaded. Be alert and drive defensively.

At Franklin Camp, we'll take the east turn onto the Bamfield Road, coming in from the Nitinat. If you're driving down from Port Alberni, you'd take the west access to the Bamfield Road by keeping straight ahead on the south side of the Coleman Creek bridge. The route goes up a hill and soon drops down a long grade into the Sarita River Valley. At km 14 (mi 8.7) you'll reach Sarita Lake. There are some nice B.C. Forest Service recreation sites on this lake. One is near the confluence of Central Creek and the Sarita River. I've spent a few days at the site just around the corner from where the tiny creek draining Bewlay Lake enters the larger Sarita Lake. Sarita Lake holds cutthroat trout, Dolly Varden (char) and kokanee. Fishing is productive in all seasons except winter. Best times are the late spring or early fall.

On one trip, an angling buddy and I spent a few hours working the lake. We trolled near creekmouths, tried bait and bobber near the dropoffs and cast a variety of lures toward likely lies — all to no avail. Another fisherman passed us by in a small cartop boat. As he puttered by, he raised his shoulders and arms, signalling that he, too, was striking out that evening. Despite the absence of tight lines, we had an enjoyable paddle along the western fringes of the lake.

You can canoe to the west end and travel down to pristine falls on the Sarita River. Don't try to navigate them though. The terrain directly to the north is steep and rises sharply to a height of 935 m (3067 ft). Such topography can funnel winds creating rough water conditions on Island lakes. While Sarita Lake is relatively small, paddlers shouldn't take it or any other wilderness lake lightly.

The next day we took off for some backwoods browsing. We attempted to find the logging road visible on the mountain directly across from our camp. Access to this spur had been choked off by thick underbrush, but we ventured onto a newer road and were able to see Sarita from a more westerly vantage point.

An employee in a MacMillan Bloedel pickup truck was coming down the slope as we were going up; we mentioned to him that we were on a photo outing and inquired if the route we were on was an active area. (We hadn't noticed any restricted access signs, but we wanted to make sure we weren't where we should not have been.) He told us that the company had been blasting a new section of road through farther up the valley, and to watch out for some heavy machinery parked in that vicinity. Other than that, he said there was no problem.

He then pulled out some photo enlargements he happened to have with him, of some elk he had discovered in a logging slash. Shot with a telephoto lens, the pictures showed the animals lying down and running up a logged-off hill. He wouldn't reveal the exact location of the pictures, but he did say that the elk had returned to their resting ground the next time he had gone up that way.

We had cut off the Bamfield Road about 6.5 km (4 mi) from our Sarita Lake camp. The main road swings due south at the junction to cross a wooden bridge over the South Sarita River. Our turnoff went north, over the Sarita River.

The next spur we went up was the winding switchback that climbs Mount Blenheim. There is a microwave facility at the top. The Mac/Blo worker also had told us that we wouldn't have any trouble on this road. (We were in a four-by-four pickup with lots of clearance.) There were some good viewpoints on the way up and after a final bumpy section, we reached the summit and a spectacular vista. The water traffic on Alberni Inlet was visible as well as the seascape near Tzartus and Fleming Islands of the Chain Group. The tidal flats at the mouth of the Sarita River, and the open Pacific to the west made good subject matter for photographs. Directly to the north was Uchucklesit Inlet, leading in to Kildonan, one of many ports of call for the *M.V. Lady Rose*, out of Port Alberni. Snow-capped peaks to the north (the most distant being part of Forbidden Plateau) and the telltale rocky crown of Mount Arrowsmith to the east made up one of the best panoramic views of Vancouver Island's natural splendour that I have yet discovered on my Island adventuring.

We weren't alone on Mount Blenheim; an employee from Bell Canada was troubleshooting at the microwave installation. He pointed out some of the immediate landmarks — San Mateo Bay and the Consinka Lakes among others — and told us of yet another viewpoint that he felt was even more impressive than the one we were taking in. He then diagrammed the route for us on one of our maps. An exploration of this locale has been ear-marked for a future visit to the Sarita/Bamfield area.

It's about 6.7 km (4.1 mi) up Mount Blenheim from the bridge at the

The spectacular vista atop Mt. Blenheim: looking north to Uchucklesit Inlet and the distant snow of Forbidden Plateau.

Bamfield Road cutoff. This road is definitely unsuitable for anything but a four-wheeler or high-slung vehicle. The grade is steep and the rocks sharp and loose. Some outdoorsmen might consider the round-trip hike up and back. This would be an arduous climb, but the sights at the top are worth the effort.

At km 27.6 (mi 17) turn right and follow the signs for Poett Nook marina and RV and tent campsite on a protected cove at the south end of Numkamis Bay. This facility is a favourite base camp for countless salt-water anglers and boaters who frequent the waters of nearby Barkley Sound.

Just over the 30-km mark (18.6 mi) is the left turn for MacMillan Bloedel's Central South mainline. This route skirts the east side of Frederick Lake and runs east to become Flora Main. Let's take a quick look at the alternate way in or out of the Bamfield area. Several other mainlines angle off Central South Main: Klanawa and Upper Klanawa are two. We once explored the Klanawa Main (after working hours) up to a bridge that was being built on the west fork of the Klanawa River. The way the forest industry is opening up new roads for timber harvesting, many newer spurs now exist in the region.

From the turn near Frederick Lake, it's 33.8 km (21 mi) to where Flora Main intersects the Cowichan/Alberni mainline. (See **Trip 10**.) Along the way you'll pass several lakes — Rousseau, Crown and Flora — the latter with a picnic and camping site along its south shore.

If you do decide to travel this route, take note that there are many secondary spurs and side roads that seem to be the mainline; it's easy to take the wrong turn. Be sure you have good maps with you and that you can understand them. The region is also travelled by industrial traffic and hauling is frequently ongoing along this narrow road. Check with MacMillan Bloedel prior to your trip. (See **Contacts**.)

The Bamfield Road goes along the west side of Frederick Lake and near Pachena Lake. Anglers can seek out the access roads to these two lakes for cutthroat and rainbow trout fishing. Cartoppers can be launched at either of these lakes and there is a picnic site at Frederick Lake. The north end of the West Coast Trail terminates at Pachena Bay. This turn is at km 41 (mi 25.5), on the left. Even if you're not planning an excursion on the trail, a stop at Pachena Bay and its exceptional beach is worth considering.

From here it's about 5 km (3 mi) to Bamfield. Watch for an original West Coast Trail footbridge on the right side of the road. This span was moved to its present location and is a point of interest. The road ends on the east side of Bamfield Inlet. Half of this tiny west coast community is on the west side of the water, so anyone travelling to Bamfield should take the time to explore both sides of the inlet. A ferry service is available to visitors.

Some of the many highlights in the Bamfield area are the Marine Science Research Centre, the trails down to Cape Beale and the great salt-water fishing. And of course, there's the West Coast Trail - - a wilderness jaunt we undertake in **Trip 13**.

Contacts:

MacMillan Bloedel (Franklin Camp) (604) 723-9471; B.C. Forest Service (Port Alberni) (604) 724-9205.

Maps/Guides:

Recreation and Logging Road Guide to Tree Farm Licence No. 44 (east map)(MacMillan Bloedel); *The West Coast Trail and Nitinat Lakes*, (Sierra Club of B.C.); *Pacific Rim Explorer*, (Obee/Whitecap); *Guide to Forest Land of Southern Vancouver Island*; Topographical Maps: Regional Map No. 2 *Parksville/Tofino* (1:125,000); 92C15 *Little Nitinat River* (1:50,000); 92C14 *Barkley Sound* (1:50,000); 92C/NE *Nitinat Lake* (1:125,000).

Nearest Services:

Port Alberni; Bamfield.

Trip 15: The Nanaimo Lakes Region

In Brief:

The Nanaimo Lakes region features a chain of lakes (First, Second, Third and Fourth lakes) in the Nanaimo River Valley. A number of additional lakes may be reached via secondary gravel roads. This is fine mountain scenery and excellent seasonal fishing. Spur roads will intrigue backroaders. Wilderness camping is possible at most lakes. This area has great paddling territory.

Access:

From Highway 1 at Cassidy take Nanaimo Lakes Road west to First Lake. Gravel roads start from this point with paved sections on the mainline. Secondary roads are gravel; may be rough and require a four-by-four. There is restricted-access in active logging areas.

Description:

Every year, an angling buddy and I get together to plan out our annual fishing trip. Our biggest problem is deciding where to go. We haul out maps, reminisce about previous hotspots; laugh over jaunts on which we've been skunked, and eventually, following numerous cups of hot coffee or several mugs of a cooler beverage, decide on a destination. One setting that we've visited more than once on our piscatorial pursuits has been the Nanaimo Lakes region. As well as the fishing opportunities and great scenery, a myriad of backroads criss- cross these woodlands.

Accessibility is rather straight-forward. Starting from the Nanaimo Lakes cutoff on Highway 1 (in Cassidy), you'll immediately come upon the intersection of the Nanaimo Lakes Road and South Wellington Road. We'll mark this junction as km/mi 0 for this run.

The road to the First Lake is paved, somewhat hilly and winding in

80

places. At km 16.7 (mi 10.3), a road to the left goes into MacMillan Bloedel territory along the South Nanaimo River Valley to the Jump Lake reservoir. This is within the Nanaimo Water District's jurisdiction. Public entry is limited in this area; however, the Nanaimo Fish and Game club mans the gate at the main road during the hunting season from 8 a.m. to 6 p.m.

The gravel mainline is reached at km 21 (mi 13). A watchman's shack and gate are located at km 22.5 (mi 14.0). If the watchman is in, normally you'll be asked your destination and length of stay. This procedure is a safeguard against theft and vandalism which has been an unfortunate occurrence in many Island backwood locales. It's a fact that a small minority of fools continue to be responsible for the restricted access policies in some areas: limitations that apply to all outdoorsmen, the majority of whom have respect for the woodlands and practice low-impact camping procedures.

You can stop in at the Fletcher Challenge office near First Lake (km 25.7/mi 16) and pick up an area brochure. A little beyond the office, watch for a signposted side road on the left. This is the turn for the wilderness campsite on First Lake. Where this secondary road crosses the Nanaimo River turn left again for the campground. We've based here in the early spring when the cutthroat trout action heats up in First Lake. The section of the Nanaimo River connecting First and Second lakes is a great canoeing stretch, all except for the rocky shallows where the river enters First Lake. This part of the river is productive for fly-casters in the early season.

The mainline (now pavement again) continues west to follow the north shore of Second Lake. There are some cottages along the lakeshore here. Just over the 31-km mark (mi 19), near the end of Second Lake, a logging road angles off to the right. This road goes up the Dash Creek Valley to Panther (Healy) and Echo (Shelton) Lakes. It can be rough, especially near Deadhorse Creek where seasonal runoff washes out the roadbed almost annually. The road begins a wide curve westward as you near the access road for Panther. The Echo Lake turn is a little before the Panther cutoff, on the left. This is Branch C-26, but the marker may be missing. It's just over 11 km (about 7 mi) to Panther Lake from the turn on the mainline, near Second Lake.

Angling in Panther Lake is limited to artificial flies. There are natural boat ramps at both Panther and Echo lakes. The fishing regulations often change from year to year, so it's a good idea to check on annual restrictions, in the *Freshwater Fishing Guide*. We've been in to Panther Lake a number of times over the years. On a clear day the majestic crown of Green Mountain forms a beautiful backdrop for Panther Lake.

On one trip, as we were fishing at our favourite spot, my partner had a fish on his line; however, the wily trout tangled the leader around our anchor rope and shook free. That episode is still brought up over coffee, usually

Whether you're casting for trout or for rugged scenery, Panther (Healy) Lake is a gem.

when we're planning our next outing. On another trip, my buddy and I were using the same model of fly rod, the same line, same reel and identical fly pattern in our fishing attempts. Obviously, though, our presentations were different, or maybe the rainbow just didn't like me — final tally: partner, seven fish; myself, nothing over the three-day outing. That situation has happened to almost everyone who fishes. It is frustrating at the time but makes for a good laugh at gatherings in the off-season.

Third Lake, smallest of the Nanaimo Lake chain, is situated near Rush Creek, just off the main road. The access road is on the left. There is a picnic site at this lake which is designated as a "kids only" fishing pond.

About 45 km (28 mi) from the start of our run, a spur road veers off to the left for Fourth Lake. The wilderness campsites here are yet another popular destination for travellers in the Nanaimo Lakes region. There is a dam at the lake's east end. Backroaders can explore some of the old roads in the Sadie Creek area near Fourth Lake. Deteriorating road conditions from lack of maintenance may make such forays suitable only for four-by fours. That, of course, doesn't prevent you from hiking around the area, as many people choose to do.

Up until the early eighties, you could follow the mainline west of Fourth Lake and drive to the north of Mount Hooper to hook up with logging arteries in the Nitinat River Valley. You could then continue on to the west end of Cowichan Lake. Such a loop is impossible now as the Redbed Creek bridge in the valley has been removed as it was unsafe for vehicular traffic. Sections of the switchback descending from the Nitinat summit near Fourth Lake are in horrendous shape from lack of upkeep and could prove impassable, even with a four-wheeler.

In early 1987, the provincial government established the Haley Lake Ecological Reserve near Haley Lake, south of Green Mountain. Vancouver Island marmots, on the endangered species list, inhabit this area. The Nanaimo Lakes district is also home to elk, deer, bear and cougar. Beaver ponds are found in several locations. And, as many backwoods browsers know, the region is also known for its great fishing.

Contacts:

Fletcher Challenge (Nanaimo Lakes) (604) 754-3206 (weekdays)/ (604) 754-3032 (weekends and holidays); Nanaimo Fish and Game Club (604) 754-2846.

Maps/Guides:

Nanaimo Lakes Road Guide, Fletcher Challenge); *Guide to Forest Land of Southern Vancouver Island*; Topographical Maps: 92F1 *Nanaimo Lakes* (1:50,000); 92G4 *Nanaimo* (1:50,000); 92F/SE *Port Alberni* (1:125,000).

Nearest Services:

Cassidy Area, Nanaimo.

Trip 16: Victoria to Parksville

In Brief:

The majority of Vancouver Island residents live in cities and towns on the Island's east coast. Highways 1 and 19 are the connecting links to these population centres. Many well-known provincial parks, such as Rathtrevor Beach, are just minutes from the main roads. Backroads galore intersect the highways, offering wilderness seekers a variety of travel choices. Points of interest are varied and rest stops are many; and there is excellent scenery all along the route.

Access:

Mile 0 of the Trans Canada Highway is located near Beacon Hill Park in Victoria and runs to Nanaimo. Highway 19 starts in Nanaimo and heads north to Parkville and beyond. The roads are paved public highways.

Description:

This trip describes the run from Victoria to Parksville on Highways 1 and 19. As you'll see, there's a lot to see and a variety of places to visit. For a change, the route follows paved highways — but you just might decide to explore some of the backroads along the way.

Starting at the Colwood overpass (km/mi 0) on the western outskirts of Victoria, it's just under 10 km (6 mi) to the parking area and picnic shelter at Goldstream Provincial Park. This is a great place to view the salmon spawning in the fall. Those planning on camping at one of the 160 serviced campsites in this park should turn left onto Sooke Road and follow the signposts to the campground. You can follow trails down to the park's picnic area. There is a network of hiking paths within the park to choose from.

Niagara Falls is located in Goldstream Park. Not the world-famous cascade, but the one on Niagara Creek where the stream catapults over a sheer mossy cliff into a deep canyon pool. A trail wends up to the falls which are impressive to see after heavy rains. Watch out for the spray!

Near the top of the Malahat is the road (on the left) for Spectacle Lake Provincial Park. Look for the signposted turn at km 20.5 (mi 12.7). Spectacle Lake is named for its shape — similar to a pair of spectacles. A trail winds around the perimeter of the lake. Swimming is a popular activity here over the summer. The lake has been stocked with Eastern brook trout, a fact known to avid fishermen. A majestic view of Finlayson Arm can be seen from the Malahat Summit pulloff, just down the road. Two more viewpoints follow in quick succession: the Arbutus Lookout and the one directly across from Brentwood Bay. On a clear day you can gaze over to Haro Strait and further east to the snowy crown of Mount Baker in Washington state.

Those with four-wheelers might consider attempting a run up to Oliphant Lake, on the Malahat Ridge. Two roads, near the entrance to Bamberton Provincial Park, climb up to this lake. These old roads are usually in bad shape, full of waterholes and washouts. Some of the steeper hills may be impassable. Watch for these routes on the left, a little before the provincial park entrance. A second option is to hike in to Oliphant Lake along trails extending from the Spectacle Lake area. Make sure you carry maps with you — Oliphant can be tricky to locate.

At km 33 (mi 20.5) you'll reach the Shawnigan Lake turn in Mill Bay. This is the road to take if you're contemplating the backroads drive to the Williams Creek Bedspring Suspension Bridge. This unique curving span is situated along the gravel roads that once linked Shawnigan Lake with the Port Renfrew area. (See **Trip 5**.) You can cut off Highway 1 at the 40 km (24.8 mi) mark and journey in to Cowichan Bay, a scenic alternate drive through rolling farmlands near Duncan. There is a boat ramp at Cowichan Bay utilized by salt-water anglers who try their luck in area salmon waters.

The road to Bright Angel Park on the Koksilan River is at km 43.8 (mi 27.2). Turn left onto Koksilah Road and follow the signs to the park entrance. A big feature here is the suspension footbridge over the river and the riverside trails. The park is a fine picnicking destination with tables and a covered barbeque pit.

Highway 1 drops down a hill to cross the Koksilah River just south of Duncan. A left at the light at the Allenby Road intersection (km 49.6/ mi 30.8) is the turn for the Cowichan River Footpath's Glenora trailhead. (See **Trip 8** for complete access details.) Then it's over the silver bridge in Duncan. The banks of the Cowichan River near this bridge is lined with steelheaders in late December and January. That's when the steelhead are in the river scooping up salmon eggs on the river bottom.

The highway passes the Cowichan Community Centre, landmarked by the world's largest hockey stick and puck. You can't miss the giant stick, originally a display at Vancouver's Expo '86. North of Duncan is the B.C. Forest Museum and its many displays on B.C.'s forest industry. Kids will enjoy a ride on the steam train that runs through the museum property. Two good trout lakes are close to Duncan: Quamichan and Somenos lakes. Both these lakes contain cutthroat and rainbow trout. The lakes are great paddling grounds for day outings.

Highway 18 meets Highway 1 at km 55.8 (mi 34.6). This road is the gateway to Cowichan Lake. See **Trip 9** for a description of the loop tour around Cowichan Lake. Another alternate drive can be made by turning right at the Crofton cutoff, north of Duncan. From here you can wend your way through Westholme and up to Chemainus; or south to Crofton. Chemainus is one of the smaller communities on the Island's east coast worth visiting. In recent years, the town has become famous for the murals adorning many of its buildings.

At km 68 (mi 42.2) a left onto MacMillan Bloedel's Cowichan Division Copper Canyon mainline leads along the Chemainus River Valley to a wilderness park. There are no facilities here. Swimming holes in the river are popular with summer explorers. Note that access is restricted on the mainline.

The community of Ladysmith is situated on the 49th parallel. This town has some of the steepest streets of any community on Vancouver Island. North of Ladysmith you can make a right onto Cedar Road (km 80.5/mi 52.8) and journey along backroads that lead to Quennell Lake, with its many arms, and Holden Lake. You'll be driving east of the Nanaimo River and eventually will reconnect with the main highway south of Nanaimo.

In Cassidy, the Nanaimo Lakes Road meets Highway 1 at km 90 (mi 56). This paved road runs to the Nanaimo Lakes region, a favourite with hunters, fishermen and backwoods browsers. Beyond the first lake in the chain, is a gravel backroad network. Access from First Lake can be restricted. (See **Trip 15**.)

The parking area for Petroglyph Provincial Park, just south of Nanaimo, is right on Highway 1. Here, short trails lead in to a series of rock carvings dating back thousands of years. These ancient drawings will intrigue both the young and old. As you drive through Nanaimo, watch for the signs indicating the turn for the Newcastle Island ferry. This ferry takes foot passengers over to Newcastle Island, a marine park accessible only by boat. There is a campsite there and many trails to explore. The island was once a producer of coal and two quarries operated there years ago. The ferry dock is right behind the hockey arena.

The **Departure Bay B.C. Ferry** terminal is in Nanaimo. Travellers heading to Vancouver and back from up-Island points often journey to the

Rathtrevor Beach is one of Vancouver Island's most expansive on the east coast.

mainland on one of the many sailings from this ferry terminus. Highway 1 (Trans Canada) runs to the Departure Bay terminal; Highway 19 (Island Highway) begins at this cutoff and heads the rest of the way up to North Island locales.

The Long Lake rest stop at km 109.2 (mi 67.8) is a nice picnicking and swimming location. Kids will enjoy feeding the ducks that frequent lake waters. As you drive along the edge of Nanoose Bay, you'll be treated to a fine view over to the north side of this salt-water bay. Just down the road (if the weather is clear) is a brief glimpse of the craggy peaks of Mount Arrowsmith in the Port Alberni region.

Backroaders and fishermen will want to note the 129.5 km (mi 80.5) mark of this trip. This is where MacMillan Bloedel's Northwest Bay Main cuts across Highway 19. This gravel mainline is the primary access road to a number of lakes and secondary roads in the hills northwest of Nanaimo. Some spurs may be unmaintained and rough, suitable only for high-slung vehicles or four-by-fours. Notable fishing lakes in this region are Boomerang, Blackjack and Kidney lakes. Most of the stocked lakes in these woodlands contain cutthroat or rainbow trout; some have both species. A viewpoint on Mount Denson can also be accessed via these backroads. Check with Mac/Blo concerning access restriction. (See **Contacts**.)

Just north of the Northwest Bay cutoff is the Parksville bypass to the Long Beach Highway (No. 4). This is the usual route taken by those coming from the south Island heading to Port Alberni. We'll keep straight ahead for Parksville. One of the most popular family camping destinations on the Island is Rathtrevor Beach Provincial Park (km 133.7/mi 83). There are 174 serviced campsites at this large park and a picnic area — both in a glade of Douglas fir. The beach is the park's big attraction. At low tide, a wide expanse of gently sloping sand is exposed, ideal for beachcombers. Sand dollars can be found almost everywhere on the sandy flats. The shallowness of the water makes high tide a good time to wade or swim in the sun-warmed waters. The park has a sani-station for recreational vehicles and another big plus — hot showers! Interpretive park programmes are available over the summer. A fee is charged from April to October. Arrive early to ensure a campsite.

At km 136.7 (mi 85) of this run is the junction of Highway 4 and Highway 19. Long Beach travellers will turn left here for the scenic drive to Pacific Rim National Park. (See **Trip 17**.) Those heading further up-Island keep straight ahead on the Island Highway. For a look at the jaunt from Parksville to Campbell River, see **Trip 23**.

Contacts:

Ministry of Parks (Victoria) (604) 387-5002; Public Information Officer (604) 387-4609/387-3940; MacMillan Bloedel (Cowichan Division) (604) 246-4714; MacMillan Bloedel (Northwest Bay Division) (604) 468-7621; Local Chambers of Commerce and Travel Infocentres.

Maps/Guides:

Hiking Trails Vol. I, (Outdoor Club of Victoria); *Recreation and Logging Road Guide to the Cowichan Division* (MacMillan Bloedel); *Guide to Forest Land of Southern Vancouver Island*; *Outdoor Recreation Map of B.C. No. 15:* (Greater Victoria-Gulf Islands-Nanaimo Region), (Outdoor Recreation Council of B.C.); Topographical Maps: 92B12 *Shawnigan Lake* (1:50,000); 92B13 *Duncan* (1:50,000); 92G4 *Nanaimo* (1:50,000); 92F1 *Nanaimo Lakes* (1:50,000); 92F8 *Parksville* (1:50,000); 92B/NW *Victoria* (1:125,000); 92F/SE *Port Alberni* (1:125,000).

Nearest Services:

Various communities along the route.

Trip 17: Parksville to Long Beach

In Brief:

The beauty of the Long Beach area is widely known; and the drive west from Parksville, through Port Alberni to the Pacific Rim National Park is equally impressive. The highway is close to two riverside provincial parks (Little Qualicum Falls and Englishman River Parks), skirts Sproat Lake, snakes through mountain passes and runs along the wide expanse of Kennedy Lake on its way to the west coast. Logging roads go in to Maggie Lake, Toquart Bay and the Kennedy River.

Access:

From Highway 19 near Parksville, take Highway 4 to Port Alberni and continue west to Long Beach. This is a paved highway with some steep inclines and winding sections. Secondary roads are gravel; they can be bumpy. Restricted access in active logging areas.

Description:

The lure of majestic strands of golden, sandy beaches and wild, breaking waves draws thousands of visitors annually; the majority of them over the warmer months. The drive into the region from Parksville along Highway 4 is a highlight in itself. You pass by Sproat Lake, climb through mountain defiles, twist your way along scenic woodlands; catch glimpses of rivers surging in deep gorges, skirt the shores of Kennedy Lake and finally emerge in the Long Beach area.

We'll begin our run in downtown Parksville, where Highway 4 Intersects Highway 19. (Note. Don't confuse this starting point with the Parksville bypass south of this community.) The turnoff to Englishman River Falls Provincial Park is at km 5 (mi 3). There are 105 tent and RV sites here. The waterfall and river ravine intrigue countless visitors at this serviced family campsite. This park takes on a different look over those rare winters when freezing weather brings an extended cold snap to parts of the Island. Then, the falls here are locked in an iron grip of ice, with only a slender trickle of water revealing any river flow. Hummocks and mounds of ice cover the rocks in the riverbed, giving the cascade a surrealistic look.

Little Qualicum Falls Provincial Park is reached by turning right at km 18.2 (mi 11.3). The river features swimming pools and a gravel beach. Avoid the area below the waterfalls; treacherous currents make swimming here dangerous. There are over 90 camping spots at this location. A daily fee is in place from April to October.

Soon you'll be driving alongside Cameron Lake, bounded by steep mountains. Two picnic sites are found along this lake's south side: the Cameron Lake Picnic Site and the Beaufort site about halfway along the lake. Several trailheads to the Mount Arrowsmith area start in this area. Cameron Lake is popular with sailboarders and anglers. Just beyond the western end of Cameron Lake is Cathedral Grove and its grand stands of virgin Douglas fir. The largest trees here are around 800 years old. Trails wind through this aging forest of giants taking visitors seemingly backwards in time.

The steep climb up the pass to the Alberni Summit (385 m/1230 ft above sea level) is next. Once at the top it's back downhill to the outskirts of Port Alberni. This bustling mill town is situated at the head of Alberni Inlet.

Our route passes the Stamp Falls Provincial Park cutoff (signposted) which you can take as an alternate way to the backroads through the Ash River Valley. Around the 50-km mark (31 mi) Mission Road meets the highway right after the bridge over the Somass River. This is the turn for those looping around Sproat Lake. Great Central Lake Road runs in to Great Central Lake and the start of the backroad network northwest of Port Alberni. (See **Trips 18, 19, 20 and 21.**)

Sproat Lake Provincial Park (km 57.5 /mi 35.7) is another popular family campground with 59 sites, a nice beach area, a boat launch and dock. A trail in the southeast section of the park goes down to some petroglyphs near the lake. You might decide to drive along Lakeshore Road near the park entrance and travel along to Bomber Base Road. Here, the Martin Mars water bombers, used to combat Island forest fires, are stationed. You can arrange for a tour of the facility; but not during the fire season.

Following the north side of Sproat Lake, you'll be treated to excellent views of this large body of water and the majestic mountains bordering its shores. Sproat Lake has four arms and is an ideal location for canoeing and kayaking. Just under the 67-km (42.5-mi) mark of this trip is Taylor Arm Provincial Park. There are 60 wilderness campsites here. The park is open from April to October and there is no fee. There are comfort stations and

The beauty of Kennedy Lake as viewed from its northwest shore.

forest trails at this locale. Look for a road on the left at km 68.5 (mi 42.5) that goes down a hill and through a small gravel pit. This leads to a picnic site (no camping allowed) on the north shore of Sproat Lake. The turn is unmarked at the highway cutoff.

At km 78.2 (mi 48.4) an industrial road intersects Highway 4. By turning left here you can drive to the B.C. Forest Service Taylor Arm wilderness campsite, a small but pretty camping spot near the mouth of the Taylor River. There is a dock here and a natural boat ramp. Many Long Beach travellers are not even aware of this tiny campground located just minutes from the highway.

A rest stop and fisheries lookout is west of the end of Sproat Lake (km 86.8 /mi 53.8). This is a good place to have a short break before tackling the mountain section of our run. The Taylor River has formed a very deep pool at the lookout and if you climb up a steep trail and look down into the pristine water below, more often than not you'll detect the shape of a resident fish, lurking amid the river's sunken boulders. An information signpost next to the parking area describes the types of fish common to Sproat Lake and gives some historical background. Picnic tables are located nearby. Right across the bridge near the rest area, an industrial road crosses the highway. You can turn left here and hook into the Sproat Lake South Shore Road. (See **Trip 19**.)

Highway 4 climbs up through Sutton Pass (the summit is 175 m/575 ft above sea level). It was in this region on a spring jaunt to Long Beach that I encountered some of the thickest fog I have ever seen. The route now snakes through towering mountains. The deep canyons of the Kennedy River will soon be visible on the right. An excellent riverside pulloff is on the right just

91

over the 100-km (62-mi) mark. Here you can walk out onto water-scoured rocks to observe the river pouring through a chute. On one trip, I was driving by this spot following a period of heavy rains. I had never seen the Kennedy River so high. Roiling rapids of turgid whitewater tossed spray and mist into the air as the swollen river exploded into its flood stage.

The road passes an eastern arm of Kennedy Lake where there is a natural boat ramp. Then it's up via the switchbacks, past tiny Larry Lake to an expansive vista of Kennedy Lake. If you're driving, you won't be able to take in much of this view; the road cliff-hugs its way down to lakeside via a twisting, narrow stretch that will require your full attention. As the highway levels out to run alongside Kennedy Lake, look for a logging road on the left that begins to parallel the road at km 125.2 (mi 77.8). This is the backroad to Toquart Bay. Let's take a side trip to this beautiful west coast beach.

Anglers may want to try their luck fishing at Maggie Lake (8.4 km/5.2 mi from the highway). The lake holds cutthroat, rainbow and steelhead. There is a tiny pulloff on the right and a natural boat ramp. It's just under 16 km (10 mi) in to the B.C. Forest Service Recreational Site at Toquart Bay. This campsite is a favourite with RV'ers who line the beach and form a mini RV city over the summer. Canoeists and kayakers launch from here and head out into the bay en route to the Broken Island Group in Barkley Sound. Salt-water anglers frequent the waters of Toquart Bay in their pursuit of salmon and other fish. A local Indian band maintains a nearby store for the convenience of Toquart Bay campers. The road in to Toquart Bay is all gravel with the usual bumps and potholes. Some sections are prone to washouts, especially in the early season, but normally access is no problem.

Back on Highway 4, you'll pass a natural boat launch along Kennedy Lake before swinging inland. On a January run one year, a friend and I spotted a group of five or six otters cavorting on a wooden raft out in the lake in this area. By the time I had parked and zipped over to a vantage point for some photos, the sleek animals had returned to the chilly lake waters and were gliding west.

At km 131.5 (mi 81.7) the access road (on the right) for Kennedy Lake Beach meets the Long Beach road. This is a popular swimming area during the summer. The beach is sandy and situated in a pocked cove on Kennedy Lake. No camping is permitted.

MacMillan Bloedel's West Main logging road crosses the highway at km 135.9 (mi 84.4). You can turn right here and drive to some great paddling areas off the beaten track. The falls on the Kennedy River are another point of interest. Let's take another side trip. West Main hits Grice Bay Main at km 8.6 (mi 5.3). The latter goes into the woodlands east of Wickaninnish Bay. Kennedy River Road (km 11.3 /mi 7.0) runs along the west side of the

Kennedy River. You can follow secondary roads around to a viewpoint near Kennedy Cove. West Main crosses the Kennedy River on a long, wooden bridge. On the far side, the road splits; Lost Lake Road is to the left; Clayoquot Arm Road is to the right.

By keeping to the right, you reach a natural boat launch just before another rickety bridge. This is the spot paddlers head out from for exploration of island-dotted Clayoquot Arm (part of Kennedy Lake) or an excursion into the main part of Kennedy Lake. Straight ahead, the logging road goes into a restricted logging area. A left at the junction will take you along Lost Lake Road to the spur angling in to the Kenn Falls trail. You'll pass West Clayoquot Main and Muriel Ridge Main en route. A backwater of the Kennedy River which looks like a small lake will appear on the left; then, 5.6 km (3.5 mi) from the junction is the overgrown road to the falls trail. Fallen trees and waterholes sometimes restrict driving along the old logging raod. You might want to park on the shoulder of the mainline and walk about 10 minutes or less to the small clearing and turnaround at the trailhead. The path drops down through a cedar forest to the rushing waters of the falls.

From the West Main intersection on Highway 4, it's only 1.6 km (1 mi) to a "T" junction. Ucluelet travellers cut left here; those going to Pacific Rim National Park and Tofino bear right. It is here that we'll end our run along Highway 4. And while the beaches of Long Beach may be your ultimate destination, there's certainly no lack of outdoor adventure possibilities on the drive in.

Contacts:

Ministry of Parks (Victoria) (604) 387-5002; Public Information Officer (604) 387-4609/387-3940; Superintendent-Pacific Rim National Park (Ucluelet) (604) 726-7721/726-4212; MacMillan Bloedel (Estevan Division) (604) 724-4477; MacMillan Bloedel (Sproat Division) (604) 724-4433; B.C. Forest Service (Port Alberni) (604) 724-9205.

Maps/Guides:

Pacific Rim Explorer, (Obee/Whitecap); *Hiking Trails Vol. II*, (Outdoor Club of Victoria); *Recreation and Logging Road Guide to Tree Farm Licence No. 44* (east and west maps), (MacMillan Bloedel); Topographical Maps: 92F4 *Tofino* (1:50,000); 92F3 *Effingham River* (1:50,000); 92F6 *Great Central Lake* (1:50,000); 92F7 *Horne Lake* (1:50,000); 92F8 *Parksville* (1:50,000); 92F/SW *Kennedy Lake* (1:125,000); 92F/SE *Port Alberni* (1:125,000).

Nearest Services:

Parksville, Port Alberni, Ucluelet, Tofino.

Trip 18: Great Central Lake/Della Falls

In Brief:

An excellent outing on Central Vancouver Island is the paddle down Great Central Lake and the hike up the Drinkwater Valley to Della Falls. This awe-inspiring cascade is the highest in Canada and the sixth highest in the world. Canoeists and kayakers will find excellent big-lake paddling on Great Central Lake; and although tenting spots along its shores are limited, the outcrops of land that are suitable for wilderness camping make good stopover points. Travellers can base at the head of the lake and day hike to the falls. Backpackers can hike up to the site of an old sawmill and explore the area from there.

Access:

Launch Points: Ark resort: take Great Central Road (west of Port Alberni) to the foot of Great Central Lake. (See **Trip 20.**) This is a paved road.

B.C. Hydro station: cross the bridge at the foot of Great Central Lake and follow the Ash Main logging road to Branch 83. Stay on this spur to the hydro station. This is a gravel combined-use road. (See **Trip 20.**)

Description:

One of the more satisfying outdoor adventures on Vancouver Island is the amphibious outing down Great Central Lake and up the rugged trail to Della Falls, in southern Strathcona Park. Great Central is an excellent canoeing lake and the falls trail leads in to the highest waterfall in Canada — the sixth highest in the world.

You have the option of two launching points. You can take Great Central Road, west of Port Alberni, to the foot of Great Central Lake and start your journey from the Ark Resort. For a small fee you can park your car here and travel the full 36.8 km (23 mi) length of the lake to the trailhead. A

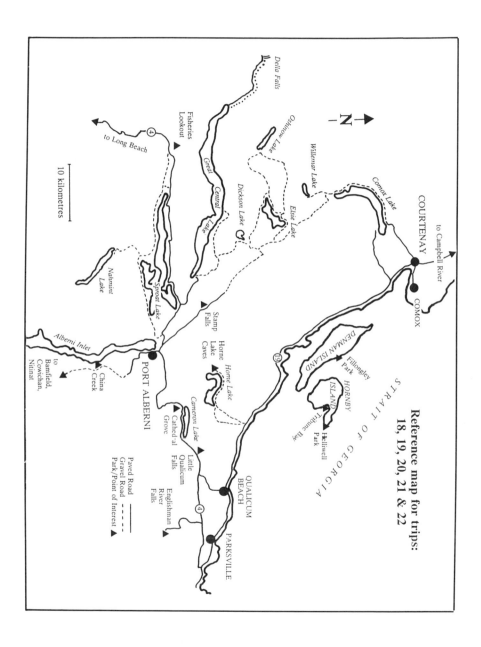

water-taxi service is available over the summer at the Ark Resort to take visitors to the start of the trail. You can also rent canoes here.

The second launch point is accessed via Branch 83, which cuts off the Ash River logging mainline.(See **Trip 20** for details.) This secondary road runs along the north side of Great Central Lake (with some great viewpoints on the way) and eventually drops down to the lakeside at a B.C. Hydro generating station near Lowry Lake. There is a tiny B.C. Forest Service wilderness campsite at this small lake.

Great Central Lake is one of the deepest on Vancouver Island with depths in places of over 330 m (1082 ft). The lake's Indian name is *moo-hulth* meaning burned-off face. The lake is dammed at its foot. As a result, there are many deadheads and sunken trees along the shoreline that can be potential hazards for paddlers. Despite these dangers, it's best to stay close to shore when the wind and waves are up. Great Central is usually windswept by the early afternoon in the summer. It's best to start your paddling just after dawn. Great Central Lake is extremely narrow at its foot. The topography is steep bordering the lake and when the winds are funnelled through the constricting mountains, paddling conditions can be tough. The lake widens out as you head west and is at its widest in the vicinity of Thunder Mountain. There are a number of islands in this area that are interesting to paddle around.

Fishing can be good at the creekmouths. Anglers work the dropoffs at these points with bait and bobber, spinning lures, or flies. Best fishing times are in the spring and fall. If you're not in any great rush to reach the head of the lake, you can slowly work your way to the west end over a couple of days, camping at wilderness sites found on points of land you'll pass by.

When you're canoe-camping, you can bring along a lot more equipment than you would were you only backpacking. Those extra luxuries, such as an ice cooler and extra food can be quite handy on an extended excursion.

West of the hydro station, there are some floating cabins on the lake and a logging workyard near Clark Point. Clark Point is an excellent stopover site. Farther west, another jut of land, identified by a stand of dead trees, provides water travellers with a second choice of tenting locations. We've stopped here for a couple of days enjoying the scenery; and — since it was extremely hot — we spent a good deal of time swimming. The lake drops off abruptly in a series of rock ledges, making this a great place for a cooling dip. These locations are on the north side of Great Central. There are other primitive campsites along the south shore you can stop at also. Look for a level spot in one of the lake's small bays where streams enter the lake.

As you near the lakehead, you'll notice some old railway trestles in the shoreline shallows. A stand of dead trees at the west end of the lake is close to a cabin and dock. A second, smaller float is situated just behind the first

Canoeists take advantage of Great Central Lake's winds.

landing, in the next bay. You can set up a base camp in the clearings near the Della Falls trailhead. No doubt some reshuffling of gear will be required prior to your falls hike.

We discovered the fickle nature of Great Central's winds on one of our trips. No two days displayed the same pattern. You can never really be sure of the wind conditions on Great Central Lake. While west winds are the prevailing ones, for two days we noted that an east wind got up by mid-morning, turning to westerly by late afternoon. Some nights it was calm; on others, the winds and whitecapped wave-trains were rolling all night. Some paddlers will take advantage of the winds and rig up a sail to catch the gusts of wind. We've seen groups of canoes sailing by, lashed together for greater stability. It's a fun way to travel, and much less tiring on the arms.

A lone kayaker passed our campsite early one morning. As he glided by, he remarked how much easier it was to make good time when the wind was down. Other travellers were whisked by our site in the water-taxi.

In the last few years, upgrading of the falls trail has been carried out. Tricky creek crossings have been bridged and the upper sections of the route have been cleared, in the vicinity of the falls. This has taken away the danger and adventure for some, but such is progress. Most of the improvements were done through the Port Alberni Regional District in conjunction with the Ministry of Parks.

Don't take a hike to Della Falls lightly, though. Washouts still make some of the creeks rough areas to traverse. The fast-growing vegetation along the trail makes it easy to miss the main route at some points. This is a wilderness setting and hikers should be prepared for the same.

The Della Falls Trail follows Drinkwater Creek along an old logging railway grade. It's a steady, but not unpleasant rise in elevation in this first section. Swamper's Marsh is located in this area, and at times — July is known to be a bad month — the mosquitoes can be ferocious here. Only an ample application of an extra-strong repellent will ward off their frenzied attacks. June visitors may find snow on parts of the trail. Even into July and August, you may encounter snow pockets slowly deteriorating in shadowy rock crevices. August can bring the best weather for hiking to the falls, but their flow may not be at its best.

The steepness of the path will slow down your pace in a couple of stretches. In these areas, each stream provides a welcome drink of cool water. After one sharp rise, hikers can look back to see an eagle's eye view of the valley just hiked through. At one point you'll come upon some huge boulders and large caverns near the creek. There is a gravel bar nearby where you can set up camp. Take care to not be caught by a sudden rise of creek waters. We camped here overnight and day-hiked to the falls the next day. That night, a thinning of the mosquito population was noticed with an increase in the no-see-ums.

A most prolific plant in this region is the Devil's Club. The Haida Indians considered this shrub's berries inedible; however, they did rub them on their heads to add a sheen to their hair. The needle-like spines of this plant can cause a severe allergic reaction for some people.

The trail crosses Drinkwater Creek on another of the newer bridges and then over two rockslides. At one of the suspension bridges you can catch your first glimpse of Della Falls, dropping over a rocky bluff. The waters tumble 439 m (1440 ft) in a series of three drops before fanning out on a rocky slope.

A sawmill once stood in the vicinity of the falls. Only decaying floors are left now, and scattered about the forest floor are rusted tools and even an old saw blade. This is where there are some good camping spots. Confort stations have been set up nearby. On a large tree, hikers have nailed boards with their names carved on them. This "tree of signs" is an area landmark to visitors past and present. A steep switchbacking trail begins near the sawmill and climbs the slope on the west side of Love Creek. This stream originates in Love Lake. From this challenging path, you can look across the valley to Della Falls. Further along, experienced climbers can follow the routes to Mount Septimus and Mount Rousseau.

From the sawmill site, you'll climb towards the base of Della Falls. There is more Devil's Club to move through and finally you reach the bottom of the falls. Photographs and words cannot describe a close sighting of the sixth highest waterfall in the world. The cold spray can be savoured relief if you've been hiking in hot weather. There is a trail of sorts which scales the left side of the falls up to Della Lake. We haven't tried this route but we have run into some travellers who had. They told us that by the time they were halfway up, they began to question what they were doing.

Della Falls was named by Joe Drinkwater, after his wife. Joe had mining claims in the region around 1911. He and his brother constructed the first road into Great Central Lake.

On my most recent trip up to Della Falls, Vancouver Island — in fact, most of the Pacific West Coast — was under the influence of a ridge of high pressure, resulting in clear skies and hot temperatures. Despite the good weather, on the afternoon we hiked down from the falls to the lakehead, thunderstorms were developing. One lightning bolt started a small fire right across the lake from the Della Falls trailhead. The blaze was quickly attended to by a helicopter with a water bucket. One of the Martin Mars water bombers, based on nearby Sproat Lake, surveyed the scene for awhile and then droned off. The tricky terrain at the fire scene necessitated the employ of a second helicopter and bucket rather than the larger aircraft. The Della Falls Trail is about 16 km (10 mi) long. Visitors should be in reasonably good physical shape, prepared for a climb of 825 m (2076 ft), and geared for a wilderness environment. Canoeing to the head of Great Central Lake and taking the Della Falls Trail is an exhiliarating adventure into a rugged wilderness, culminating with a look at one of the true marvels of nature on Vancouver Island.

Contacts:

B.C. Hydro (Port Alberni) (604) 723-3551); MacMillan Bloedel (Estevan Division) (604) 724-4477; Ark Resort (604) 723-2657; B.C. Forest Service (Port Alberni) (604) 724-9205; Ministry of Parks (Victoria) (604) 387-5002; Public Information Officer (Victoria) (604) 387-4609/387-3940.

Maps/Guides:

Recreation and Logging Road Guide to Tree Farm Licence No. 44 (east map) (MacMillan Bloedel); *Hiking Trails Vol. III* (Outdoor Club of Victoria); Strathcona Provincial Park Brochure (Ministry of Parks); Topographical Maps: 92F5 *Bedwell River* (1:50,000); 92F6 *Great Central Lake* (1:50,000); 92F7 *Horne Lake* (1:50,000); 92F/SW *Kennedy Lake* (1:125,000).

Nearest Services:

Port Alberni Area.

Trip 19: Sproat Lake Loop Drive

In Brief:

You can circle the four arms of Sproat Lake, west of Port Alberni, by following logging mainlines on the south side and Highway 4 on the north shore. Wilderness campsites are numerous on the southern fringes of Sproat Lake and one logging road cuts into the mainline to climb sharply up to Gracie Lake and south along the shores of Nahmint Lake. The tiny Taylor Arm campsite near the mouth of the Taylor River is popular with anglers. Sproat Lake Provincial Park and a picnic site are accessed from the highway.

Access:

Follow Highway 4 west from Port Alberni to the bridge over the Somass River. Turn left onto Mission Road. Logging roads are gravel mainlines (combined-use). Secondary logging roads may be rough. Active logging may restrict travel in some areas.

Description:

Sproat Lake is situated to the west of Port Alberni. There are over 160 km (100 mi) of shoreline on the lake, which is comprised of four arms: Klee, Stirling, Two Rivers, and the one visible along the Long Beach highway, Taylor Arm. The Sproat and Somass rivers connect Sproat Lake with the Alberni Inlet. Sproat Lake was named in 1864 (after Gilbert Malcolm Sproat) by Dr. Robert Brown, one of the principal members of the Vancouver Island Expedition of that year. This excursion scouted out Island resources for possible development. The Indian name for Sproat Lake is "Klee-coot", roughly translated as "wide open". History records that early natives may have believed the lake was haunted. They did not live in the vicinity although they did fish its waters.

A 75-km (50-mi) loop tour around Sproat Lake is possible by taking logging mainlines around the south side and Highway 4 on the north side. The starting point for this drive is Mission Road. Keep on the Long Beach highway as you pass through Port Alberni. You,ll drive down River Road, alongside the Somass River. Mission Road is the first left after the bridge over the river.

The turn for the J.V. Clyne Bird Sanctuary is about 1.6 km (1 mi) from the cutoff. This tidal flatland is home to a variety of waterfowl, including Canada's largest, the trumpeter swan. These birds usually arrive at the estuary in November to winter there through March. Naturalists are able to view the swans in their natural habitat. The MacMillan Bloedel Sproat Lake Division offices are just down the road from the bird sanctuary. On weekdays you can pop into the office and inquire about current hauling activities.

The first section of the Sproat Lake loop runs down Stirling Arm Main. You'll pass a small roadside pond called Devil's Den Lake. Around the 14-km (mi 8.5) mark look for the access road for Fossli Park. Hiking trails lead from the parking area to the lakeside where you'll find a fine, developed beach. Stirling Arm Main then skirts Two Rivers Arm. Many outdoorsmen are familiar with the wilderness campsites along this scenic arm of Sproat Lake. Some vacationers launch a boat in this vicinity and transport tent and gear over to the northeast side of the arm. On summer runs along the mainline, you'll see their camps across the lake waters.

Just over the 21-km (13-mi) mark is the left turn for Gracie and Nahmint lakes. If you decide to explore this route, you'll soon find yourself climbing high into the mountains. Two or three pulloffs are located near Gracie Lake, known for its spring and fall rainbow-trout fishing. A steep, but short trail leads down to the lakeside. The road continues by Gracie Lake to run along the east side of Nahmint Lake. This lake holds cutthroat and rainbow trout. Wild steelhead are also found in Nahmint. Anglers should check the fresh-water fishing regulations carefully for current restrictions concerning wild steelhead.

You can follow the road to a viewpoint near Nahmint Bay on Alberni Inlet. From here you can swing north along the inlet to a campsite and boat launch near Macktush Creek. There is another campsite further north almost directly across the inlet from China Creek Park. Near Cous Creek, the logging road cuts inland to head south of the Arbutus Summit and eventually hooks back into Stirling Arm Road near the Sproat Division offices.

Sproat Lake tourers swing north beyond the Gracie Lake road and then west along what is now called South Taylor Main. Several active logging roads are in this region: Riverside, Nahmint and View mainlines. South Taylor Main drops down to the lakeshore at several points. Along one stretch, you'll be driving by some cliffs. There are some narrow, blind corners in this area, so keep a watch for other traffic on the road.

Dad attends to dinner at a B.C. Forest Service wilderness campsite on Sproat Lake.

If you're travelling during wet weather, the mountainsides in the Sproat Lake area explode with instant waterfalls, as runoff waterways carry excess precipitation to the streams and rivers. The rivers rise quickly. Such a scene is a stark contrast to the one on a dog-day summer afternoon. Two creeks on South Taylor Main with pretty falls are Antler Creek and Snow Creek. Just west of the Snow Creek bridge is a side road (on the right) going in to a boat launch and B.C. Forest Service wilderness campsite. This site is on Taylor Arm, near the mouth of the Taylor River. Fishing can be excellent in this arm of Sproat Lake. Sproat Lake contains cutthroat and rainbow trout as well as kokanee and coho salmon.

At km 40.4 (mi 25) you'll reach a wooden bridge over the Taylor River. You can cut right here and continue along the gravel secondary road to a Highway 4 access or to the wilderness campsite on Taylor Arm's north side. There is a boat launch at this locale and a limited number of camping spots. We'll stay on South Taylor Main and continue our westward drive. This last section of the mainline meets the Long Beach highway at a rest stop and fisheries lookout on the Taylor River.

Before you reach this point of interest, you'll drive through a region that was devasted by the 1967 Tay Fire that raged through the woodlands.

This fire was accidently started by a spark during road construction. An estimated 70 percent of the timber was salvaged and the area was successfully replanted. Grim evidence of the fire remains on the mountainsides: burned trunks of trees still standing on some slopes.

On one February trip to Long Beach, a friend and I were venturing down this part of the backroads. The freezing level, which had been marked by fresh snows on the hillsides to our left, suddenly dropped to roadside, creating a damp curtain of rain and wet snow. At first, the large, wet flakes melted as they hit the ground; soon, however, the snow was beginning to build up on the roadway. Luckily, I had good winter tread tires on my vehicle.

The fisheries lookout is an excellent place for a break or a picnic. Trails lead to river lookouts and there is an information signpost with area history and data on species of fish common to the region's waters. Turn right at the rest stop and head east for Port Alberni. This leg of this jaunt goes along the north side of Sproat Lake. Several viewpoints and provincial parks are located near Highway 4. (See **Trip No. 17** for details.)

You might decide to turn onto Lakeshore Road as you near the outskirts of Port Alberni for an alternate drive where there are private campsites and resort facilities. The base for the Martin Mars water bombers is accessed from this road.

A lot has changed in the Sproat Lake area since the days of the early settlers. Logging roads snake up adjacent mountains and valleys and the Long Beach highway is travelled by countless holidayers each year. And yet, as you stand on the shore of a clandestine cove on Sproat Lake, listening to the lonesome cry of a loon reverberate over the waters, you might conclude that, somehow, nothing has really changed that much after all.

Contacts:

MacMillan Bloedel (Sproat Division) (604) 724-4433; B.C. Forest Service (Port Alberni) (604) 724-9205.

Maps/Guides:

Recreation and Logging Road Guide to Tree Farm Licence No. 44 (east and west maps), (MacMillan Bloedel); Topographical maps: 92F7 *Horne Lake* (1:50,000); 92F2 *Alberni Inlet* (1:50,000); 92F3 *Effingham River* (1:50,000); 92F6 *Great Central Lake* (1:50,000); 92F/SE *Port Alberni (1:125,000); 92F/SW Kennedy Lake* (1:125,000); Regional Map No. 2 *Parksville/Tofino* (1:125,000).

Nearest Services:

Port Alberni area.

Trip 20: Backroads: Port Alberni to Courtenay

In Brief:

The logging-road network that connects the Port Alberni area with Courtenay is a backwoods paradise of forests, lakes and mountains. The route cuts through the Ash River Valley and skirts the west side of Comox Lake to emerge in the Courtenay region. There are countless lakes for canoeing and fishing — Dickson is one favourite — and the many side roads will intrigue four-by-four explorers. Most spurs are negotiable in a regular vehicle, but even if you're stopped by rough or impassable roads, you can always hike.

Access:

Take Highway 4 to Port Alberni and head west to Great Central Road (near Sproat Lake Provincial Park). Turn right. The logging road begins at the foot of Great Central Lake. This is a gravel mainline, with some steep grades which can be rough. Secondary roads may require four-by-four. Parts of the route may be impassable over the winter. Most roads are combined-use arteries; heavy industrial traffic in some regions.

Description:

The backroads from Port Alberni to Comox Lake and Courtenay provide up-Island travellers with an alternate route to North Island points. The roads are all gravel — some mainlines and some secondary spurs — and they can be rough in places. Some hills are prone to washouts and unless your vehicle is high-slung, you can expect some scraping of the undercarriage in these problem spots. Over the winter, a few passes become choked with snow. So if you're thinking of venturing to this part of the Island in a normal car, it's best to plan your jaunt for the summer or fall.

First you have to drive to Port Alberni. Take River Road and follow

Highway 4 as if you were going to Long Beach. From the bridge over the Somass River, it's just under 7 km (4.5 mi) to Great Central Road, where you turn right. This paved road winds its way through hilly terrain to the foot of Great Central Lake. The salmon hatchery near the lake is worth a visit. From the hatchery road it's a further 1 km (0.6 mi) to the Ark Resort on Great Central's shores.

Over the summer, many outdoorsmen will park their vehicles at the Ark Resort (for a fee) and launch a canoe or kayak for the paddle down the length of Great Central to the Della Falls trailhead. (See **Trip 18**.) The MacMillan Bloedel Ash Main logging road begins near the resort. A narrow bridge crosses the Sproat River. We'll mark this span as km/mi 0 for this trip. Avoid any spur roads and stick to the mainline.

Branch 83 (on the left at km 6.5/mi 4) goes along the north side of Great Central Lake to a B.C. Hydro generating station near Lowry Lake. Some Della Falls adventurers will launch from this hydro facility. (For a detailed description of the wilderness excursion to the falls see **Trip 18**.)

The Ash mainline (a combined-use road) swings north and then west as you near Dickson Lake. Keep an eye out for a marker at km 11.7 (mi 7.3) pinpointing the trailhead for Dickson Falls. With a four-by-four you can negotiate the rugged spur road a short distance to where it peters out; or you can simply park your vehicle on the shoulder of the mainline. Make sure you're well off to the side of the roadway. It's a short hike up to the falls trail. The path crosses a rocky section of terrain and then drops sharply to the base of Dickson Falls where there is a large river pool. This picturesque cataract takes on the look of a grand staircase when the Ash River is running high.

The Ash River bridge is at km 13 (mi 8). Look to your left as you cross this span; you'll see Dickson Lake and its outlet stream, always a stirring sight for first-time viewers. The entrance to a wilderness campsite and natural boat launch on Dickson Lake is just beyond the bridge — a spur road on the left. This camping spot is a favourite with early spring fishermen who brave brisk winds and showery weather as they get in their limited hours of fishing time on lake waters.

There is a three-way junction at km 15 (mi 9.3). Some visitors opt for the left fork which goes along the west side of Elsie Lake. There is a plethora of fishing and paddling lakes in the area: Ash, Turnbull, Lowry, McLaughlin and Lois lakes. Some may require a four-wheeler to reach, especially in the off-season; others can be carefully accessed in a regular car with deft manoeuvring.

More intrepid explorers can continue beyond Elsie Lake and journey up to Oshinow (Deep) Lake in the southeast corner of Strathcona Park. You can loop back to the north shore of Elsie via the Ash River Road and Branch 110. This route passes Toy Lake and follows Ramsay Creek. (See **Trip 21**.)

View from the Ash River bridge near Dickson Lake.

If you're heading to Comox Lake, take the middle road at the three-road junction. At km 18 (mi 11), watch for the small sign indicating the sharp left turn for the Comox area. If you accidentally miss this road, you'll end up at the corner of Somers and Woolsey Roads, northwest of Port Alberni. You can reach Ash Main via this connecting artery by taking the Stamp Falls turn in Port Alberni. This follows Beaver Creek Road down to the entrance to Stamp Falls Provincial Park and on to the Comox road link. A stop at the provincial park is worth considering. A visit is highlighted by deep gorges and the Stamp Falls. Along riverside trails you can hike to excellent vantage points from which to watch the spawning salmon in the fall.

The Alberni Economic Transportation Committee is promoting an alternate up-Island corridor running from Cowichan Lake, Nitinat Lake to Franklin Camp and north to Port Alberni; from here the proposed route goes in to Comox Lake and on to Courtenay. You'll see signs marking this road link along many Island backroads.

The next leg of this jaunt passes Pear Lake and descends a series of hills. At this point, you'll be driving to the east of the Beaufort Range of mountains. There are private cottages situated along the east shore of Comox Lake. A little before these dwellings, the road curves left to cross the Toma Creek bridge. Farther along you'll come upon a "T" in the road. This is the

Willemar Lake turn. (See **Trip 22** for a look at a paddling adventure in the Willemar region.)

Keep to the right at the "T" for Comox Lake access points and Courtenay. About 5 km (3 mi) from the Willemar road is the cutoff for Old Camp Point, right before the Cruickshank River bridge. The left spur is usually in the best shape although the hill can be challenging coming back up. The right side road is steeper and the rocks are loose. Old Camp Point is a disused logging camp and former booming ground. It was once the terminus for logs driven down the Cruickshank River. In its operating days, the camp housed loggers, their wives and children. A schoolhouse was located there as well. At Old Camp Point you can drive to the mouth of the Cruickshank River and try some shorecasting. The river has eaten away part of the roadbed, which once extended farther out into the lake.

The wooden bridge, high over the Cruickshank River, displays signs of its age: in a couple of places the planking has deteriorated, necessitating makeshift improvements, no doubt put in place by fellow backwoods browsers and area cabin owners. A weight limit is now in place and the bridge approaches have been modified with wooden guides to restrict the size of vehicles crossing the span. Don't worry, though; the bridge is safe.

Reset your odometer at the Cruickshank bridge. On the north side of the river, the road ascends a hill. This grade is prone to washouts and a high ridge of gravel in the centre of the roadway could play havoc with low-slung vehicles. This washboard hill can be extremely bumpy. Its condition depends on the amount of road maintenance the Comox Lake Road has received, whether from area cottage owners or the region's logging firm, Fletcher Challenge.

There are a number of up and down sections to drive as you head northeast towards Courtenay. Spur roads on the right provide access to Comox Lake. At times, the road clings to sheer cliffs high above the lake waters. It is in these areas that travellers will see panoramic vistas of Comox Lake and the surrounding mountains. The road cuts inland to hairpin corners with cascading streams directly at roadside. Approximately 11.5 km (7.mi) from the Cruickshank bridge is the last long hill on the route. Yet another expansive Comox Lake view can be seen at the top.

Watch for the signpost indicating the left turn to the B.C. Hydro dam and picnic site at the top end of Comox Lake. The dam regulates water flow from the lake to the Puntledge River. The turnoff for this point of interest is at km 14.2 (mi 8.8). Eventually, the road levels off at the bridge and causeway at the top end of the lake. The gravel ends soon. From here it's just a matter of following the road to Lake Trail Road, which runs into Courtenay.

You can take the Island Highway in Courtenay to head to points further north. You may prefer more logging road adventuring and opt for the backroads from Courtenay to Campbell River instead. (See **Trip 24** for an account of these backroads.)

Contacts:

Fletcher Challenge (Courtenay) (604) 334-3105; MacMillan Bloedel (Estevan Division) (604) 724-4477; MacMillan Bloedel (Sproat Lake Division) (604) 724-4433; B.C. Forest Service (Port Alberni) (604) 724-9205.

Maps/Guides:

Logging Road Guide, (Courtenay area), (Fletcher Challenge); *Recreation and Logging Road Guide to Tree Farm Licence No. 44* (east map), (MacMillan Bloedel); Topographical Maps: 92F7 *Horne Lake* (1:50,000); 92F11 *Forbidden Plateau* (1:50,000); 92F6 *Great Central Lake* (1:50,000); 92F/SE *Port Alberni* (1:125,000); 92F/SW *Kennedy Lake* 92F/NW *Buttle Lake* (1:125,000).

Nearest Services:

Port Alberni, Courtenay.

Trip 21: Backroads: Elsie Lake/Oshinow Lake Loop

In Brief:

Backroad enthusiasts who prefer to travel to more remote areas will enjoy the loop drive up to Elsie and Oshinow (Deep) lakes, northwest of Port Alberni. There are fishing lakes, great scenery and excellent paddling waters in this neck of the woods. Best of all is the fact that you can circle trip on these backroads — but can you resist the temptation to explore some of the secondary roads?

Access:

Take the Ash River mainline from the foot of Great Central Lake to the three-way junction just beyond Dickson Lake. (See **Trip 20.**) The route is a gravel mainline. Some sections of this combined-use road may be rough. Secondary roads may require a four-by-four. Snows may block sections of the route over the winter.

Description:

An interesting backroads loop that I try to make at least once a year starts along the Port Alberni/Courtenay logging road network. (See **Trip 20.**) The route follows combined-use mainlines. You may encounter industrial traffic at certain times. Check with MacMillan Bloedel prior to setting out for updated hauling information. (See **Contacts.**)

Drive through Port Alberni and head west on Highway 4. Turn right onto Great Central Road. At the foot of Great Central Lake, turn right onto the logging road and cross the bridge. From this point, it's about 15 km (9.3 mi) to the three-way junction where we'll start our run.

Take the left turn onto Ash River Road and reset your odometer to zero. You'll cross the Ash River bridge right after the turn. This is the section of the Ash River that pours out of Elsie Lake. A quick glance to the left will reveal Dickson Lake, off to the west. You can cut onto a secondary spur (on the left) a little ways along that goes to Ash Lake. A couple of tiny wilderness campsites here are used as base camps by fishermen. By taking the road that runs along narrow Ash Lake, you can reach the north end of McLaughlin Lake. Cartop boats, canoes and kayaks can easily be launched into this lake for paddling or fishing outings.

This road then runs south to pass Lois Lake and eventually arrives at the shore of Lowry Lake, where there is a natural boat launch at the B.C. Forest Service recreation site. All the lakes in this region contain cutthroat and rainbow trout. They are popular fishing spots with Port Alberni locals.

The Ash River Road skirts Turnbull Lake, a long, slender and relatively shallow body of water. On one trip through, a friend and I noticed a great deal of bug activity above the lake waters. We didn't have our fly rods along on that trip, but Turnbull looked like a fine choice for some fly-casting. The road starts to climb beyond Turnbull Lake. In the off- season this section can be rough, with gravel ridges in the centre of the roadway. At the top of one hill is an impressive vista looking out over McLaughlin Lake; and to the south, Lois Lake. Way off in the distance is a sliver of Great Central Lake. We,ve often stopped at a roadside pulloff to take in this spectacular view. If you look closely, you'll be able to see the penstock that carries water from Elsie Lake, over hilly terrain to a B.C. Hydro generating station on Great Central Lake. It is from this hydro facility that many Della Falls venturers will launch. (See **Trip 18**.)

Next comes Elsie Lake, the area'a largest lake. Elsie Lake is dammed at its east end, providing a water source for the B.C. Hydro system. Boat launches may be found on the southwest and north shores of Elsie. Near the west end of Elsie Lake is the southeast boundary of Strathcona Provincial Park. The road soon crosses the Ash River once again. You might want to stop and take in the scenery on either side of the bridge. It's a pretty spot and well worth taking the time for a few photos.

Branch 124 angles from the mainline to wind east along the north shore of Elsie Lake. Stay on the Ash River Road for Oshinow Lake. You'll now be travelling up a narrow valley hemmed in by steep mountains. There are some Ash River pools that can be reached along this part of the drive. Avoid any side roads in this region. One spur crosses the Ash River near the south end of Oshinow Lake. The main road will swing to the right to the span over the stream draining Toy Lake. A tad farther along, watch for another spur to the left that backtracks to Oshinow.

Oshinow Lake is also known as Deep Lake. It is a long, thin alpine lake with three wilderness campsites on its northeast side. These are separated by a sloping beach area. A friend and I once spent three days camped at the

Breathtaking scenery awaits those who travel to Oshinow Lake.

lake, spending our time fishing and canoeing. We were fortunate to have no rain during our late June stay. The mountain scenery from our camp was magnificent as we took in the snow-capped heights of the Red Pillar and the lofty ridges beyond, all within the Comox Glacier Nature Conservancy Area.

On the first night, we set up camp, had a quick bite to eat and launched out for the evening bite. We saw lots of fish sign, but didn't luck into any that evening. We tried several possible hotspots, including the mouth of the creek coming down from Toy Lake, to the north. That night, the stream's gurgle lulled us to sleep.

The next day, we loaded up the canoe and slowly began trolling our way to the head of Oshinow Lake. The highlight of our paddling foray was the sighting of a series of waterfalls tumbling over a high ridge on the lake's north side. Each began as a thin line of water at the top of the bluff. These fanned out over some rocky ledges to cascade down sheer cliffs towards the lakeshore. You normally hear these falls well before you see them.

The Ash River pours into Oshinow at the lake's northwest end; the source lies at Tzela Lake, west of the Cliffe Glacier. We canoed up the shallows to a set of rapids. Here, we zipped across the current to a quiet back eddy and ate lunch in the shade of the riverside trees. It had been a scorcher all the way down Oshinow and we welcomed the cooling shadows. We drifted back to camp a little later, still attempting to entice the elusive trout with our offerings of worm and lures. At one point we were buzzed by a bee who proceeded to pester us for some time before finally departing.

When we landed back at our campsite, it was decided that a swim was in order. Well, it may have seemed hot in the canoe and on the shore, but the glacier-fed waters of Oshinow Lake were not quite as warm as we expected. Nevertheless, we did go in and were refreshed after a somewhat-abbreviated dip.

That night, the bite came on again and we hooked into a couple of rainbow trout. These went into our cooler for breakfast the next day. We added a few more to our total the next morning and enjoyed a hearty meal of trout — lightly fried in butter and garlic. There are cutthroat and rainbow trout in Oshinow. We found the bite to be sporadic. It could come on at any time, even high noon. The lake waters might be calm, wind-riffled or even wavy when the cry of "Fish on!" was heard. I opted for bait and bobber; my partner was adamant in his use of spinning lures. Both methods proved successful.

During one lull in our fishing exploits we headed over to the outlet of the lake — the section of the Ash River we had seen on an initial search for the Oshinow access road. That's when the wind really picked up, even though it was getting near sunset. This was the roughest water we had to deal with during our visit.

Despite the fine weather we encountered, we didn't see any fellow travellers until we were packing up to leave. That afternoon, a pickup pulled up with a camper on its box. The driver told us he had parked his trailered boat back near Elsie Lake and continued on without it in order to scout out road conditions up to Oshinow.

You can travel northeast from Oshinow to pass a series of smaller lakes: Toy, Junior and June lakes. There are some fishing restrictions which apply to these bodies of water, so be sure to check the fresh water fishing regulations carefully. Cutthroat and rainbow are found in these lakes. The road (Branch 110) follows the Ramsay Creek Valley for about 16 km (10 mi) to where that stream enters Elsie Lake. Nimnim (Long) Lake can be reached along a secondary spur just under 2 km (1.2 mi) from the Ramsay creekmouth.

Nimnim Lake is another narrow lake to the south of Mount Hennessy. In recent years, the lake has been periodically stocked with rainbow trout. Cutthroat are also present in Nimnim. Anglers have hooked into fish of 1.8 kg (4 lbs). Primitive campsites and a launch area for cartop boats makes this locale a fisherman's hideaway.

One late spring I was planning on looping through this part of the backwoods; however, I had been told by Mac/Blo employees at their Sproat Lake office that windfalls blocked the road from Toy Lake through to the

Nimnim access. Workers were slowly clearing the deadfall, working their way in from the east. It pays to check with local logging company offices for up-to-date information on hauling and road conditions prior to venturing on the backroads.

At the Ramsay Creek bridge near Elsie Lake, you can turn right onto Branch 124 and drive about 6.4 km (4 mi) to the junction with the Ash River Road. The north-shore boat ramp on Elsie Lake is along this branch road. We'll continue our loop and cut left at the Ramsay creekmouth.

The route skirts Elsie Lake's east side. You can follow a spur down to the B.C. Hydro dams on the lake, where the Ash River empties out. This section of the route is called Long Lake Road. It hooks up with the Ash River Road back at the three-road junction — our starting point for this trip. Active logging or high forest fire hazard can restrict public access along parts of this circle tour; snows can block the backroads completely when the winter brings heavy snows. These variables won't deter the many outdoorsmen who, through proper planning and timing, venture into these woodlands to take in the great scenery and superb fishing at any one of the region's lakes.

Contacts:

MacMillan Bloedel (Estevan Division) (604) 724-4477; B.C. Forest Service (Port Alberni) (604) 724-9205.

Maps/Guides:

Recreation and Logging Road Guide to Tree Farm Licence No. 44 (east and west maps), (MacMillan Bloedel); Topographical Maps: 92F7 *Horne Lake* (1:50,000); 92F6 *Great Central Lake* (1:50;000); 92F/SE *Port Alberni* (1:125;000); 92F/SW *Kennedy Lake* (1:125,000).

Nearest Services:

Port Alberni.

Trip 22: Paddling The Willemar Lake Region

In Brief:

Willemar Lake nestles in the mountains between Courtenay and Port Alberni. Beyond it lies the Forebush lake chain, near the headwaters of the Puntledge River. Here, canoeists and kayakers can camp in a wilderness setting while exploring a beautiful region of Vancouver Island. A portage trail connects the lakes which can be fishing hotspots in the spring and fall.

Access:

From Port Alberni: follow the logging mainlines from the foot of Great Central Lake to the Willemar cutoff near the south end of Comox Lake. (See **Trip 20**.)

From Courtenay: take the logging mainline that runs along the west side of Comox Lake south to the Willemar access road. (See **Trip 20**.) Roads are gravel mainlines (combined-use) with some steep hills and rough sections. The Willemar road is prone to potholes, and large puddles are common in rainy weather.

Description:

One area of the Island I have frequented over the years is the Willemar Lake region. This lake is located directly south of Comox Lake, in rugged terrain bearing appropriate names such as Rough and Tumble Mountain and the Comox Gap.

The Willemar is an excellent choice of destinations for fishermen, campers, canoeists and kayakers. The route in passes Comox Lake (if you're coming in from Courtenay); or you can journey through the Ash River Valley, near Port Alberni, to arrive at the Willemar from the south. Either way, there are some excellent viewpoints along the way and intriguing side roads to satisfy backwoods browsers.

114

We decided to come in on the gravel roads from the north, so a quick long distance phone call to the Fletcher Challenge (then called Crown Forest) office in Courtenay gave us two key pieces of information: there was no active hauling in the area, and no fire closures were expected for at least two or three weeks.

The Willemar access road is about 5 km (3 mi) south of the Cruickshank River bridge on the Alberni/Courtenay backroads. (See **Trip 21**.) From this junction, it's a simple matter of following the spur to Willmar Lake's shores. The way in can be bumpy and there may be waterholes to contend with.

I've been at Willemar Lake in the heat of the summer, when even the chilling glacial waters of the Puntledge River felt good. Oft times I have been there in the off-season, as chilling fall winds brought drizzle and rain to the area.

On one trip, rather than using my aluminum canoe, a friend and I journeyed in with his kayak. He brought along his two-man Folbot model, a good stable craft for bucking the waves that the Willemar might throw at us. Willemar Lake is not as large as Comox Lake, yet it is bordered by tall mountains; terrain that can funnel winds and create steep wave trains. Paddlers with open canoes should be wary when the wind gets up.

By the time we had off-loaded at the boat launch at Willemar, the drizzle had increased to a moderate rain. We quickly stowed our gear in the kayak and launched out into the lake, carefully tucking the spray skirts around us. There were other campers near the boat launch, utilizing one of several wilderness campsites located close by. In past visits, I'd noticed the natural beauty of the area had been tarnished by careless campers who had thoughtlessly left garbage and debris strewn around. It was good to see things had changed. More and more people are now practicing low-impact camping and actually cleaning up their sites, leaving them tidy for the next visitors. Only one other craft was out on the lake — a canoe carrying a pair of anglers trolling with fly rods. They told us they were having some success near the creekmouths, using a shrimp imitation on a sinking line.

Willemar was singing with the fall of rain as we began our paddle down to the western end. At the halfway mark, the skies really opened up. It was still pouring as we landed at the wooded wilderness campsite, close to where the Puntledge River enters the lake. We hastily set up a large fly, under which we erected my geodesic dome tent. These dome-design tents are a great improvement over the old, square models. They require far fewer pegs; they are set up quickly and can be moved around; and they stand up better to high winds. Once the tent was in place, we proceeded to cook dinner on a tiny pack stove and settled in for a damp evening under the fly. We harboured hopes that the rain would let up by morning.

Boaters survey the waters of the Puntledge River mouth, at the western end of Willemar Lake.

There are a fair number of deadheads in Willemar Lake that drift up and down its length at the whim of the winds. Those that wander near the mouth of the Puntledge River are often caught in an incoming current, swept up at a great speed to become snared by a large back eddy that forms in this area. If the wind is steady, these water-snarled rogues can be pushed up against a lee shoreline, sometimes to be crowded up 12 deep or more.

We awoke one morning to discover that our camp's water access was completely choked off by these deadheads. The log blockade later thinned out as the wind died and the flow from the Puntledge carried some of the logs back out into the lake. As it was, we still had to forceably shove a few stubborn strays away so that the kayak could be launched.

All along parts of Willemar Lake's shoreline stand tall, dead skeletons of trees, some grim reminders of the passage of a forest fire. Over time, they will fall and add to the deadfall in lake waters. Other deadheads are the result of logging activities from years gone by.

Willemar Lake has many moods. One afternoon we watched the calm lake turn into a windswept fury of confused waves in the course of only ten minutes. The long, narrow shape of the Willemar and its precipitous mountain boundaries had combined with sudden gusts of high winds to produce these rough water conditions.

In late May of 1983, a major storm (occurring at the end of a hot spell) hit the Comox/Willemar area. Some cabin owners said it was the worst storm in 20 years. Wharves on Comox Lake were destroyed by heavy waves, which at one point were reported as 1.8 m (6 ft) high. Part of the road near the south end of that lake was washed out. Such can be the nature of the region's weather.

We saw our fishing friends a couple of times over the next few days as they slowly trolled the Willemar shoreline, with apparent continued success. One hotspot they had found was on the south shore, near the Nimnim creekmouth. This creek drains Nimnim Lake and cascades over a falls near the logging road on Willemar Lake's east side. At one point, the anglers shipped their fishing rods and prepared for an attempt at paddling up the Puntledge River, to the start of the Forebush lake chain, a little way upriver.

In a short while they were back at the river mouth, having run into a frisky upstream current that eventually negated their paddling efforts. The section of the Puntledge connecting the lake chain with Willemar Lake was still running at an elevated level. In the drier summer months, paddlers can line up the channel and easily reach the Forebush Lakes.

We also tried to get into Forebush via the river. At first the going was easy in the broad shallows at the river mouth; up around a bend, however, the waterway narrowed and the current became more pronounced. Our forward progress diminished while our paddling became more intense. About a third of the way up, it became apparent that we would have to abort our endeavour. After resting a few minutes and wiping perspiration from our faces, we let go of the anchoring branches we were holding onto at riverside, and spun around to be hurriedly caught up by the current and swept back to the wider part of the river.

The portage trail, on the left bank, is a short distance upstream. If the Puntledge is too high for travel, adventurers must use this access to the Forebush lakes. At the west end of the Forebush chain you can seek out a trail leading hikers through a virgin forest at the headwaters of the Puntledge River. Fishermen will relish the solitude as they test the lake waters. At certain times of the year, there is great fishing action in this region.

The waters of Willemar Lake right out from our campsite exhibited a constantly changing parade of deadheads that wandered wherever the Puntledge current shifted them. As evening shadows stole out over the lake, numerous risers were heard. Telltale widening rings, spreading out on the darkening lake surface, pinpointed the location of feeding fish. We found sunset to be the best time to cast out for the trout. We had to be precise with our aim, having to contend with the forever varying positions of floating logs. One slight error could lead to a snagged lure or hook — and the loss of terminal tackle.

The wilderness campsite at the Puntledge River mouth is an excellent spot to view conflicting forces of nature. Following a steady afternoon of blowing winds, standing waves were created near the mouth as the stream's current met the wind-induced waves. These same winds can deposit deadheads in the river shallows where they could give paddlers coming down the waterway quite the surprise. With these potential dangers, it pays to be cautious.

Near the boat launch at the east end of the Willemar, the road goes by the primitive campsites and climbs the steep western fringe of Mount Hennessy. You can hike up this old road to a lofty height from which there is a postcard view looking west over Willemar Lake to the mountain glaciers beyond.

The Willemar Lake region is not really far from civilization, yet there's something about paddling below Rough and Tumble Mountain or on the wilderness waters of the Forbush Lakes that makes you think you could be miles from anywhere.

Contacts:

Fletcher Challenge (Courtenay) (604) 334-3105; MacMillan Bloedel (Estevan Division) (604) 724-4477; B.C. Forest Service (Port Alberni) (604) 724-9205.

Maps/Guides:

Logging Road Guide, (Courtenay area), (Fletcher Challenge); *Recreation and Logging Road Guide to Tree Farm Licence No. 44* (east map), (MacMillan Bloedel); Street and District Map of the Comox Valley and Surrounding Area, (Comox Valley Search and Rescue Association); Topographical Maps: 92F11 *Forbidden Plateau* (1:50,000); 92F6 *Great Central Lake* (1:50,000); 92F/NW *Buttle Lake* (1:125,000); 92FSW/*Kennedy Lake* (1:125,000).

Nearest Services:

Courtenay, Port Alberni.

Trip 23: Parksville to Campbell River

In Brief:

The section of the Island Highway from Parksville to Campbell River threads it way along the east coast of Vancouver Island. There are great seascapes in the region known as "lighthouse country." The highway is close to a number of provincial parks and the views across the Strait of Georgia over to the mainland mountains are impressive on a clear day. The ferry terminals for Denman and Quadra islands are on the route as is the road to the Powell River ferry, departing from the Comox area.

Access:

In Parksville, stay on Highway 19 and continue north to Campbell River. The route is paved with some winding corners.

Description:

The Central Vancouver Island portion of Highway 19 extends from Parksville to Campbell River, a 119-km (74-mi) jaunt to the junction with Highway 28. Set your odometer to zero where Highway 4 meets Highway 19 in downtown Parksville.

You'll pass through French Creek and then arrive at Qualicum Beach. The beachfront at Qualicum has always been a favourite with strollers and beachcombers. Summer sunsets are a treat to see from this waterfront. Much of the time, the highway follows the Strait of Georgia, with excellent scenery. Lasqueti and Texada islands dominate the view. Clears days are best for seeing the towering mainland mountain ranges.

The left turn for Spider Lake Provincial Park and Horne Lake Caves Provincial Park is at km 24.2 (mi 15), near the Horne Lake coffee shop. Spider Lake, so-called owing to its shape, is a destination for picnickers, swimmers and paddlers. No power boats are permitted on lake waters.

119

The warm, shallow waters at Tribune Bay Provincial Park on Hornby Island provide hours of fun for youngsters.

Smallmouth-bass fishing action heats up in the summer.

To reach the Horne Lake caves, you have to drive along Horne Lake to the west end. The sheer rock bluffs along the lake's north side are impressive. The caves are a little beyond the privately-owned and operated campsite at the head of Horne Lake. Vandalism has taken its toll on the caves; as a result, access is limited. Cave tours of varying lengths and difficulty are provided jointly through the Canadian Cave Conservancy and the Vancouver Island Cave Exploration Group.

Just down the road from the Spider Lake/Horne Lake cutoff is the signposted road to the Big Qualicum salmon hatchery. The best time to visit this facility is in the fall. Then, visitors can watch spawning salmon through a window below the river's surface. This hatchery is one of several operated on Vancouver Island by the Department of Fisheries and Oceans.

The next part of the route runs through what is called "lighthouse country," including such communities as Bowser and Deep Bay. Fishing resorts line the highway, catering to salmon fishing guests. Many of the private campgrounds and motels in this area offer salmon charters to visitors.

Out in the strait, Denman and Hornby islands are predominant. Around the 50-km (31-mi) mark is the ferry terminal for Denman Island at **Buckley Bay.** A second ferry departs Denman for the smaller Hornby Island. Both Denman and Hornby islands have a variety of trails for hikers. Denman's Fillongley Provincial Park is a popular destination, although there is a limited number of camping sites here. Hornby's two provincial parks — Tribune Bay and Helliwell — are day-use facilities. The warm, shallow beach at Tribune Bay is perfect for sunbathers and swimmers; Helliwell Park features a trail leading to a bluff overlooking the Strait of Georgia.

At km 66.3 (mi 41) is the left turn in Royston for Cumberland. This

A derelict ship forms part of a breakwater near Royston.

community was once a centre for coal mining. The museum in this small town near Comox Lake is filled with historical relics from the mining days. Access to the southeast shore of Comox Lake and a boat launch can be reached by driving through Cumberland and following the signs. You can camp nearby or enjoy a lakeside picnic.

An unnamed road (km 67.2/mi 41.8) cuts off Highway l9 to the right and terminates at a small turnaround and parking area fronting the waters of Comox Harbour. Offshore, next to an old log-booming ground are a number of old boats, lined up as a breakwater. We've launched a canoe (in calm weather) and paddled around the wrecks.

Courtenay is next, with its strong farming, logging and fishing background. The Forbidden Plateau region is a skiing hotbed over the winter. Summer brings in hundreds of hikers who trek the countless area trails. (See **Trip 25**.) you can take Lake Trail Road from Courtenay and head west to Comox Lake and on to the Willemar region. You can even drive to Port Alberni on the backroads. We look at this backwoods jaunt in **Trip 20**. Salt- water anglers often base in the Courtenay/Comox district for fishing vacations. The Powell River ferry terminal is located just north of Comox at Little River.

Driving north on Highway 19 from Courtenay, you'll come upon one of the routes for the Mount Washington ski area. Turn left at km 77.7 (mi 48.2) and follow the signs. The lofty heights of Forbidden Plateau mountains loom in the west along this part of the trip. Miracle Beach Provincial Park, a large 193-site, serviced facility, is at km 95.7 (mi 59.5). Turn right from the highway and continue east to the park entrance. There is a great beach at this park.

Visitor programmes are a feature of the amphitheatre over the summer. Arrive early in the morning so you won't miss out on finding a camping spot at this fine family campground. A fee is charged from mid- May to September.

Highway 19 crosses the Oyster River and passes a stretch of road along which many charter-boat rentals are available. These businesses cater to Campbell River area salmon fishermen. Campbell River is referred to as the Salmon Capital of the World. You don't even have to rent a boat to try sone casting for salmon. The new Discovery Pier in Campbell River provides a location for the kids and seasoned shorecasters to try their luck. Some good-sized fish have been caught from the pier, which extends 183 m (600 ft) out from the shore.

Just south of Campbell River is Big Rock, a huge glacier-deposited erratic left from the last Ice Age. It looks somewhat out of place on the shoreline. The hot salmon-fishing waters near Quadra Island's Cape Mudge are visible on the right as you approach Discovery Passage and the town of Campbell River. Some travellers will want to journey over to Quadra Island for a day or two. Indian petroglyphs in the vicinity of the Cape Mudge lighthouse will intrigue visitors. Beautiful Rebecca Spit Provincial Park (a marine park) has safe moorage for boaters. You can also drive in to this day-use park and walk down its long, sandy beach.

The ferry terminal for Quadra Island is located right on Highway 19, near Campbell River's downtown core. At km 119.1 (mi 74.4) you'll reach the junction of Highway 19 and Highway 28. Straight ahead goes along Highway 28 to Gold River. (See **Trip 26.**) For North Island points, turn right at this intersection and cross the Campbell River bridge. For an account of the scenic trip along Highway 19 from Campbell River to Port Hardy, see **Trip 27.**

Contacts:

Ministry of Parks (Victoria) (604) 387-5002; Public Information Officer (604) 387-4609/387-3940; Horne Lake Caves Information (604) 757-8541; Local Chambers of Commerce and Travel Infocentres.

Maps/Guides:

Topographical Maps: 92F8 *Parksville* (1:50,000); 92F7 *Horne Lake* (1:50,000); 92F10 *Comox* (1:50,000); 92F11 *Forbidden Plateau* (1:50,000); 92F14 *Oyster River* (1:50,000); 92K3 *Quadra Island* (1:50,000); 92F/SE *Port Alberni* (1:125,000); 92F/NE *Powell River* (1:125,000); 92F/NW *Buttle Lake* (1:125,000).

Nearest Services:

Various communities along the route.

Trip 24: Backroads: Courtenay to Campbell River

In Brief:

The backway from Courtenay to Campbell River is known to local anglers who frequent a number of lakes accessed along this route. The Mount Washington Road intersects the Courtenay/Campbell River arteries just outside of Courtenay. This jaunt runs through Fletcher Challenge and MacMillan Bloedel territory, there are plenty of secondary roads along the mainlines for further exploration.

Access:

In Courtenay, stay on Cliffe Avenue to First Street. Turn right, then left, and follow Condensory to Piercy Road. Go left at this intersection and continue 4.6 Km (2.8 mi) to the Fletcher Challenge Duncan Bay Main near the Mount Washington signpost. Turn right onto the mainline. The route is a combined-use gravel road. Secondary roads may be rough and could require a four-by-four. Some regions are restricted access. There is heavy industrial traffic within Fletcher Challenge forestlands near Campbell River.

Description:

The backroads from Courtenay to Campbell River run through Fletcher Challenge and MacMillan Bloedel forestlands, along mainlines which usually are nothing more than a little bumpy. Some areas are restricted access. One starting point is the Mount Washington turn from Forbidden Plateau Road, outside of Courtenay. Turn right onto the Fletcher Challenge Duncan Bay mainline. The road crosses a bridge over Browns River and continues 5.2 km (3.2 mi) to the base of the Mount Washington Road. Keep straight ahead on the mainline.

Watch for an old road on the right at km 8.1 (mi 5). This narrow road goes into Wolf Lake and a small dam at the lake's foot. This road is usually

The supports of a logging railway trestle still stand in the waters of Wolf Lake.

bumpy; in wet weather, there can be many mud- and waterholes to contend with and a profusion of potholes. Local fishermen know the spur well. A washed out road near the dam can be hiked up to a tiny lake on Constitution Hill. The dam site is an excellent location for a picnic. Paddlers and those with cartop boats can launch along the lakeshore and head off for lake exploring. The supports of an old railway trestle can still be seen in the lake waters.

Beyond the Wolf Lake access you'll be driving along a tunnel-like route bordered by a forest of second-growth timber. At km 14 (mi 8.7) you'll reach the top end of Wolf Lake. A side road cuts down to the lakeside where there is a small boat and canoe access. This part of the lake can become choked with deadheads when the wind blows from the southeast.

At km 16.1 (mi 10) turn left for Regan Lake. The road climbs up to the access road for Regan and continues to rise into the rugged Piggott Creek Valley. At one point, the mainline (Rossiter Main) curves along a cliff face with the yawning chasm of the river directly to the right of the roadway. The road into Regan Lake is similar to the Wolf Lake access — bumpy and prone to potholes and waterholes. If in doubt about any of the larger puddles, it's always a good idea to check the depth before slogging through. During wetter weather, only four-by-fours are able to negotiate the problem spots.

Duncan Bay Main heads north. The Oyster River is a picturesque sight and you can park on either side of the bridge (make sure to stay well off to the shoulder of the road) and inspect this stream on foot. Right before the bridge is a secondary road which can be explored alongside the south banks of the Oyster River. This spur hooks up with Rossiter Main at a four-way intersection near Regan Lake.

At km 31.3 (mi 19.3) is a three-road junction. Keep right here; the left road runs into active MacMillan Bloedel territory and is usually gated. At km 31.6 (mi 19.6), turn left to continue north to Campbell River. Straight ahead runs east to the Island Highway near Oyster Bay. The road passes to the west of the Campbell River airport along a relatively flat stretch. You have a choice of three routes at km 44.8 (mi 27.8): you can continue straight ahead to the western outskirts of Campbell River; turn right onto an industrial road leading to the southern edge of the city; or cut left, as I like to, and stay on the backroads until the intersection with Highway 28 near Echo Lake.

This route crosses the Quinsam River, skirts Mirror Lake to follow the south side of Echo Lake. You can reach Quinsam Lake via a secondary road that runs south from Echo Lake. Quinsam has good fishing all summer (although late spring/early fall are ideal times) and there is a campsite at the lake where cartoppers can be launched.

Near Echo Lake, you'll drive through the Fletcher Challenge Elk River Division logging yard and then reach the Gold River Highway. Turn right onto the paved road for Campbell River. It's not a long drive on the backroads from Courtenay to Campbell River, yet the route offers backroaders and fishermen a wide choice of destinations along the way.

Contacts:

Fletcher Challenge (Courtenay) (604) 334-3105; Fletcher Challenge (Elk River Division) (604) 287-7103; B.C. Forest Service (Campbell River) (604) 286-3282; MacMillan Bloedel (Menzies Division) (604) 287-8881.

Maps/Guides:

Visitors Guide (Courtenay area) (Fletcher Challenge); *Recreation and Logging Road Guide to the Forestlands of Northern Vancouver Island* (east map), (MacMillan Bloedel); Topographical Maps: 92F11 *Forbidden Plateau* (1:50,000); 92F14 *Oyster River* (1:50,000); 92K3 *Quadra Island* (1:50,000); 92F/NW *Buttle Lake* (1:125,000).

Nearest Services:

Courtenay, Campbell River.

Trip 25: Hiking Forbidden Plateau

In Brief:

When the winter snows dissipate from the lofty heights of Forbidden Plateau in Strathcona Provincial Park, hikers converge on countless trailheads ready to sample the area's alpine atmosphere. Well-defined trails make this region an excellent hiking destination featuring outstanding scenery and a choice of routes. Stocked lakes provide fine fishing action for those packing a fishing rod. You can day hike or make Forbidden Plateau the setting for a longer excursion.

Access:

Take the Mount Washington road at its intersection with Fletcher Challenge Duncan Bay Main just outside of Courtenay (See **Trip 24**). The route is a gravel combined-use road, with some steep hills and narrow sections.

Description:

The name Forbidden Plateau might conjur up images of danger and intrigue for some. Vancouver Island Indian legends tell that in times of battle with other hostile tribes, the Comox Indians would send their women and children onto the plateau to wait out the skirmishes in safety. However, when they could not be relocated after a battle with the Cowichan Indians, the area was shunned as a forbidden land. It was thought that a race of hairy giants living in the ice caves of Mount Albert Edward had tossed their victims off the sheer cliffs of the Cruickshank Canyon to their deaths.

Island skiers find the name synonymous with great skiing to be found at the Forbidden Plateau ski area and the nearby Mount Washington slopes. To hikers and naturalists, the plateau offers a series of well-defined hiking trails, signposted by the Comox District Mountaineering Club and others. These trails are close to Courtenay and give the novice hiker the opportunity to hone his skills on a day hike or overnighter into sub-alpine and alpine terrain. For the more seasoned traveller, the area offers the lure of longer treks into alpine meadowlands and the option to climb various mountains and ridges, notably Mount Albert Edward. This mountain is the highest peak on the plateau rising a towering 2093 m (6868 ft) above sea level. The view from the route up is spectacular.

I've journeyed up to Forbidden Plateau a number of times over the years, usually spending three or four days on each trip. The striking contrast of weather conditions I've encountered has always stuck out in my mind. One year, two trips, separated by only a fortnight were as different as night and day. The first jaunt, one late August, provided extremely warm weather, and I had the chance to swim in several high-altitude lakes. For the second visit, rain and fog swirled into the region, eliminating a pesky bug problem and also obliterating some of the outstanding views and vistas on the preceding excursion. Swimming was out and raingear was on.

Forbidden Plateau is within Strathcona Provincial Park. There are several access routes to the trailheads. A couple of trails begin near the Forbidden Plateau ski lodge. The Mount Becher trailhead is marked along one road leading up to that skiing facility. From its start you climb across a tangle of logs over Boston Creek and then up Boston Ridge to Mount Becher. The route is extremely steep. You can return to the starting point along an old railway bed. It was on this trail that a 75-year-old-prospector named Rees died in 1933. His affinity to the area he obviously loved is exemplified by the fact he spent most of his time out on the trails. Today, Rees Creek and Rees Ridge bear his name.

You can climb up to the summit of one of the runs at the Forbidden Plateau ski lodge and take the Becher Trail in through Slingshot Meadows and McKenzie Meadows near Douglas and McKenzie lakes. McKenzie Lake is a little over halfway to Kwai Lake, which is centrally located on the plateau. Kwai Lake is an exellent spot to base camp. Other regions of Forbidden Plateau are easily accessible from here. Time in to Kwai Lake from the ski parking lot averages around six hours. Up until 1982, you could hike up an old logging road in Cruickshank Canyon to Moat Lake, southwest of Kwai. A severe washout cut off this route which remains impassable today.

You can also travel up Mount Washington and begin your hike at Paradise Meadows, near the Nordic skiing lodge. From this starting point, it's less than one hour onto the plateau. This is the most popular approach to the area. Once through Paradise Meadows, the trail begins a climb up to Battleship Lake. You can day-hike into this lake or head over to Lake Helen McKenzie for a day outing. This route is used by cross-country skiers over the winter months. The trails are easily found and marked with ribbons. The first

Murray Meadows on Forbidden Plateau. The delicate vegetation of the meadow bog is easily damaged by the boots of careless hikers.

section of plateau paths are made of wood chips. At the south end of Battleship Lake, the trail cuts through several meadows and skirts a few tarns (small alpine lakes) on the way to Croteau Lake. You'll pass Kooso and Lady Lakes on the way.

Croteau Lake is a favourite spot for campers and can be crowded on weekends and holidays. A trail nearby goes up Mount Elma. Areas such as Croteau Lake are subject to overuse. This can be alleviated to a degree by concerned hikers who clean up and pack out a little more garbage than they pack in. A little extra effort by everyone will go a long way in preserving the delicate balance of the fragile alpine and sub-alpine regions.

Just past Croteau Lake, you'll descend a steep incline near Murray Meadows. Careless hikers have wandered from the main trail and attempted to cross the centre of these meadows. Their trail through the delicate vegetation is reflected by the mud and ooze of heavy footsteps. What might take only a second to trample requires a much longer time to recover. Hikers should make an effort to stay on the trails at all times.

Near the end of Murray Meadows, you can cut onto the Becher Trail and then take the Mariwood Lake turn. This is another picturesque body of water dotted with tiny islands. Less than half an hour beyond Mariwood Lake is the Lakes Beautiful region. This section of the plateau consists of various-sized lakes bordered by alpine vegetation. A stream connects the lakes and cascades over a falls into the largest of the chain, named appropriately enough, Lake Beautiful. The trail runs beyond the lakes and heads to Cruickshank Canyon.

Take note that insects can be a problem up on Forbidden Plateau. Mosquitoes lurk in the air along with the devious no-see-um. The coming of dawn's first light heralds the appearance of black flies and deer flies. You'll seldom be free from attack by some flying fiend. An extra-strong repellent is highly recommended as essential gear for plateau visitors.

On one trip to Forbidden Plateau four of us set out. Three of the group had previously hiked to Cape Scott, at the northern tip of Vancouver Island. One member of our hiking party was a greenhorn to the trails. The weather was chilly, drizzly and threatened to turn even more dismal according to projected forecasts. The mountain vistas and superb scenery I savoured on a previous visit were all but engulfed by the grey curtain of fog, rain and cloud.

Despite the inclemency of the weather, our spirits were high as we headed out from Paradise Meadows aiming for Croteau Lake. We made good time. Once at Croteau, we soon had our four-man tent up, a fire going and supper on the way. Another group was set up a few hills away. The blowing clouds obliterated the nearby lakeshore and the heights of Mount Elma.

We awoke the next day to steady rain and swirling fog. The other party was already tearing down their camp and soon headed back out to civilization, unwilling perhaps, to chance the fickle weather any further. At this point, we decided realistically to head up to the cabin at Kwai Lake, hoping it would be vacant and dry. It was here we based for the duration of our trip, making a series of day hikes to surrounding regions.

We were forced to rig up a ground sheet under a few leaks in the old cabin's roof. Although the walls literally ran with water all night as a result of the incessant downpour, we managed to stay dry and warm. Sleep was another matter however; our dilettante hiking companion, fresh in a wilderness environment, became fascinated with a marauding mouse, and proceeded to relate its every movement to us at regular intervals.

I convinced one member of our group to grab his fishing rod and come along on a fishing exursion to Mariwood and Lake Beautiful. The plateau has undergone a fish stocking in recent years and fly-casting can be productive. On this day, though, the wind-whipped rain and fog kept the fish hidden. We returned to the Kwai cabin via a steep shortcut trail near Mariwood Lake. At dusk, the rain subsided and we spotted some stars through the overhead canopy of clouds. Maybe a break in the weather was upon us.

Hairtrigger Lake sits up on a ridge behind Kwai Lake. On a day hike we journeyed into Hairtrigger and over to the Lake Helen McKenzie Trail where we found the cutoff to the Lake Beautiful region. In the falls area we ate our fill of blueberries that grew in profusion along the trail and near the lake. The Lake Helen MacKenzie Trail joins the main plateau trail just past Hairtrigger Lake and leads to McPhee and Circlet Lakes. Amphitheatre Lake is in behind these two. Another trail goes to Moat Lake, reported to be a hot fishing spot at certain times.

When weather conditions are right, you can climb Mount Albert Edward, crossing Mount Frink before reconnecting with the Moat Lake Trail. Beyond Circlet Lake, the Mount Albert Edward route is straight up, marked with rocks and the occasional ribbon. Eventually you'll reach a plateau which is much gentler than the first part of the trail. Hikers should note that fog and clouds can suddenly move in without warning on plateau trails. It is easy to become disoriented and lose the trail. More than one day hiker has had to spend a chilly, damp night temporarily stranded on some of the higher mountain routes.

Our first-time hiking buddy didn't set out on any day hikes on his first backpacking adventure. He seemed content to hang around the cabin at Kwai and, in his words "...keep an eye on the food in case the mouse comes back." Actually he probably wanted to watch the provisions in case he himself became a little hungry.

I suggested we hike out via the Lake Helen MacKenzie Trail and thus complete a loop tour of part of Forbidden Plateau. From Kwai and beyond Hairtrigger, the path ran through a series of meadows before descending abruptly near Mount Brooks. We zigged and zagged our way through ancient timber bordering the trail. Lake Helen MacKenzie is one of the larger plateau lakes. Piggott Creek drains the lake on its north shore. There is a delightful campsite here and this particular area is a destination for many overnight campers.

For those individuals who have never hiked in the alpine or sub-alpine regions, and for first-time hikers in general, Forbidden Plateau provides the setting for a relatively safe excursion. Using common sense and making the trip with someone familiar with the area is advisable.

Over the winter months, the trails lie silent under their covering of snow. Only the striding of cross-country skiers marks the drifts in the meadowlands. With the coming of spring and the melting of the snows, the alpine bursts into life once more, with unique wildflowers painting the landscape. That's the time hikers return to once again delight in the

The Lakes Beautiful region of Forbidden Plateau is aptly named.

outstanding scenery along the countless trails of Forbidden Plateau.

Contacts:

Ministry of Parks (Victoria) (604) 387-5002; Public Information Officer (604) 387-4609/387-3940.

Maps/Guides:

Hiking Trails Vol. III, (Outdoor Club of Victoria); Strathcona Provincial Park brochure, (Ministry of Parks); *Forbidden Plateau Trail Map*, (Maps B.C.); Topographical Maps; 92F11 *Forbidden Plateau* (1:50,000).

Nearest Services:

Courtenay area.

Trip 26: Campbell River to Gold River

In Brief:

For those who prefer to travel on paved roads, the 87-km (54-mi) trip from Campbell River to Gold River on Highway 28 is an excellent choice. This winding route goes by several provincial parks (it cuts through the northern tip of Strathcona Park), and provides access to fishing and paddling lakes, hiking trails and backroads galore. Beautiful mountain scenery highlights the run to Gold River, a lumber town with its own unique charm.

Access:

Drive to Campbell River on Highway 19. Highway 28 begins near the Campbell River bridge, north of town. This trip follows a paved highway. There are some winding sections and industrial traffic is common.

Description:

Highway 28 begins just northwest of Campbell River, where Highway 19 swings north to cross the Campbell River bridge. We'll call this junction km/mi 0 for this trip. Elk Falls Provincial Park is just down the road. Watch for the signposted entrance on the left. This large (121 tent/vehicle sites) campground is fully serviced. A fee is charged from mid-May to September. Located on the banks of the Quinsam River, it's a good spot for family campers to base while visiting the Campbell River region. A trail runs along the river to a salmon hatchery, well worth a look.

Follow the highway to the top of the big hill where you take a right turn for the day-use part of the park. Tall Douglas fir and two boisterous falls — Elk and Moose — will delight visitors. Next is the sigposted entrance for McIvor Lake, popular with swimmers, boaters and fishermen. It's really part of Campbell Lake. There are some great beaches on McIvor Lake and good boat launches.

The highway winds by Mirror and Echo lakes. You can pull off the road and park near these lakes and try shoreline casting or simply enjoy a roadside picnic. Echo Lake in particular can be a fishing hotspot. I've driven by at sunset and seen countless risers dimpling the lake waters. There is a Fletcher Challenge logging yard near the west end of Echo Lake. An industrial road intersects the highway here. A left onto this private road leads to the access road to Quinsam Lake and east to the backroad running from Courtenay to Campbell River. (See **Trip 24**.)

Argonaut Main meets Highway 28 at km 17.7 (mi 11). This industrial artery is the main access to Wokas Lake and Upper Quinsam Lake. Gooseneck Lake and Middle Quinsam can also be reached along secondary roads branching from Argonaut Main. Wokas Channel separates Upper Quinsam from Wokas Lake. There are some nice primitive campsites in this area. I've based here for fishing and canoeing outings. Upper Quinsam is a canoeist's treat with quiet coves and several islands to visit. Wave action can come up suddenly if the wind is strong; a fact to be noted by neophyte paddlers.

For those who enjoy afternoon runs on logging roads, this region has countless routes for backwoods browsers to investigate. Most can be carefully negotiated in a normal car; others require a high-slung vehicle or four-by-four. Around the 27-km (16.5-mi) mark is a hard-to-see road on the left-hand side of the highway. This goes in to Gooseneck Lake from the north. You can hook up with Argonaut Main from this spur. Backroaders can explore many side roads in this region. There are a number of small dams and spillways in these woodlands which regulate water flow in district lakes and rivers, including the Quinsam River. These are part of the elaborate drainage system which maintains water levels for B.C. Hydro power stations nearer Campbell River.

Strathcona Dam can be reached by turning right off Highway 28 at km 28.7 (mi 17.8) and heading north to the site. You can cross the dam and follow a somewhat rugged road on the far side to eventually connect with the logging-road network in the Sayward Forest region. (See **Trip 28**.) The highway curves along the east side of Upper Campbell Lake, the large body of water formed by the Strathcona Dam. The lake and mountain scenery is exceptional as you near Strathcona Park Lodge (km 40.7/mi 25.3), the well-known outdoor education centre and resort.

Soon you'll hit the boundary for Strathcona Park. Highway 28 turns right to cross the bridge at Buttle Narrows, the short waterway connecting Upper Campbell Lake with Buttle Lake. Straight ahead continues down the east side of Buttle Lake to terminate at the Westmin Resources Myra Mine. Travellers venturing down this road can camp at the 76-site Ralph River campsite and choose from a variety of area hiking trails: Wild Ginger, Karst Creek, Shepherd Creek, Flower Ridge, Myra Falls and Tennent Lake are some. On the west shore of Buttle Lake, accessed only by boat, is the Marble

Meadows Trail. This switchbacking path climbs up to alpine meadows near Marble Peak.

The Buttle Lake campsite is situated on the west side of the lake, a short distance from the Buttle Narrows bridge. Water and firewood is available here and there are 85 campsites. Kids will enjoy the adventure playground at this campground.

The highway skirts the west arm of Upper Campbell Lake. High mountains dominate the landscape in this section of the drive. The Lady Falls parking lot is on the left at km 63.9 (mi 39.7). You can park your vehicle and hike up to this picturesque cascade on Cervus Creek. The trail is short but does require some climbing up to the falls.

Hikers seeking a challenging trek will enjoy the Elk River Trail. The trailhead is at km 71.0 (mi 44). This trail follows the Elk River Valley and ascends 555 m (1820 ft) to Landslide Lake. In spots, the sheer valley walls hem in travellers. Newer bridges have replaced some tricky log crossings; in fact, some years ago, the start of the trail was relocated to avoid a crumbling section that was succumbing to erosion near a cliff- face.

In the early season, parts of the 10-km (6.2-mi) trail can be in rough shape and may require climbing over deadfall. I remember one stretch, just before a river flats, which veered down a slippery slope with fallen trees across the route. Some streams have no bridges and hikers must cross these on the rocks. A beautiful part of the trail is beyond Volcano Creek and at the top of a long hill. The path levels off here to pass the base of a waterfall whose waters pour down almostly directly on the trail.

Back on Highway 28, the road passes the Drum Lakes. These small bodies of water are another part of the hydro development servicing the Campbell River area. The water level in the lakes fluctuates periodically. Nearby is the beginning of the Crest Mountain Trail. This 5-km (3-mi) route goes up a ridge from where you can see the Elk and Heber river valleys and surrounding mountains.

You'll soon leave Strathcona Provincial Park and be nearing Gold River. This part of the drive runs along the Heber River. At km 87.0 (mi 54) you'll reach the Gold River townsite. In the mid-sixties, the town was relocated to its current location from the mouth of the Gold River on Muchulat Inlet. Canadian Pacific Forest Products Ltd. (formerly CIP), the area's major logging firm, then constructed a pulp mill where the town had stood.

Finished products from the mill are loaded directly onto sea-going ships that ply inlet waters and beyond. It's quite something to watch the loading of these vessels. Like Port Alice, west of Port McNeill, Gold River was an "instant town." It is ultra modern; neat and tidy, well planned, and has a population of over 2,000 residents. There are underground hydro and telphone facilities: as a result there are few telephone and power lines

Timber is unloaded into the saltchuck at the Gold River pulp mill.

overhead. Gold River has a central shopping core, a neighbourhood pub, a library, schools, parks and a pristine residential section.

A short drive from Gold River to the end of Highway 28 at Muchulat Inlet is worth the effort. As you reach the town limits, a signpost on the right indicates Peppercorn Park. Running along the banks of the Gold River, this town park has riverside trails of varying difficulty and a number of swimming beaches. Highway 28 follows the river valley down to the sea. Sheer rock cliffs and towering mountains make the drive a scenic delight.

The Canadian Pacific company offices are located just off the highway and visitors stopping in can pick up an area map showing logging roads and points of interest. Employees there will inform you on access restrictions along hauling roads and branch lines. This company is a leader in genetic research that leads to taller trees of better quality than ever before. Their seed orchard and research centre are located in Saanich, near Victoria.

About 2.7 km (1.7 mi) from the townsite is the Big Bend picnic site. Anglers are often seen testing the deep pool in the river. The Gold River is popular in season with steelheaders; many Gold River locals have their own favourite fishing holes. Some anglers base at the Lion's Club campsite, located nearby. As you near the pulp mill and the end of the highway, you might find the roadway lined with cars and trucks, many with boat trailers. Salmon fishing can be excellent in Muchulat Inlet; however, boaters with smaller craft should be aware of prevailing west winds which funnel up the channel. These can create heavy chop when they blow against an ebbing tide.

The terminus of Highway 28 is where the *M.V. Uchuck III* docks. This boat carries passengers to such west coast destinations as Tahsis, Zeballos and Kyuquot. The vessel, once a U.S. minesweeper, was built in Portland, Oregon in the forties.

The pulp mill is often a bustle of activity. Trucks hauling lumber line up to be quickly off-loaded into inlet waters where scurrying dozer boats boom the logs. Steam and smoke billow from the noisy mill site. The rumble of heavy machinery drones to the beat of the modern logging industry. For children and grownups alike, it's a great place to pass a couple of hours.

Backroaders may be lured up to Donner Lake. The secondary road to this lake starts near Gold River and passes Kunlin Lake before reaching the northern tip of Donner Lake. The lake is just north of Mount Donner; a little to the southwest is the towering peak of Golden Hinde, the highest mountain on Vancouver Island. Spelunkers will want to visit the Upana Caves. Gold River is the headquarters of the B.C. Speleological Federation. The Gold River area has a number of sites that can be explored. (See **Contacts**.)

From Gold River you can take logging mainlines north to Woss Camp and Highway 19. For a close look at this run, including a stop at Muchulat Lake (14 km/ 8.7 mi from Gold River) and the wilderness campsite there, see **Trip 30**. You can also return to Campbell River the way you came — on Highway 28. Should you choose this option, you'll have the opportunity for a second look at the varied and outstanding sights and scenery along the route.

Contacts:

Ministry of Parks (Victoria) (604) 387-5002; Public Information Officer (604) 387-4609/ 387-3940; B.C. Forest Service (Campbell River) (604) 286-3282; Canadian Pacific Forest Products Ltd. (Gold River) (604) 283-2221; B.C. Hydro (Campbell River) (604) 286-6288; Fletcher Challenge (Elk River Division) (604) 287-7103; Speleo Lec Tours (Gold River caving) (604) 283-2691.

Maps/Guides:

Outdoor Recreation Map of B.C. No. 6 (Campbell River Region), (Outdoor Recreation Council of B.C.); *Hiking Trails Vol. III*, (Outdoor Club of Victoria); Canadian Pacific Forest Products Ltd. Logging Road Map, (Gold River area); *Strathcona Provincial Park* brochure, (Ministry of Parks); Topographical Maps: 92K3 *Quadra Island* (1:50,000); 92F14 *Oyster River* (1:50,000); 92F13 *Upper Campbell Lake* (1:50,000); 92F12 *Buttle Lake* (1:50,000); 92E16 *Gold River* (1:50,000); 92E9 *Muchulat Inlet* (1:50,000); 92F/NW *Buttle Lake* (1:125,000).

Nearest Services:

Campbell River, Gold River.

Trip 27: Campbell River to Port Hardy

In Brief:

Port Hardy is 234 km (146 mi) north of Campbell River via the Island Highway. Communities along the way are few and far between, but there is lots to see en route. Stella, Pye and McCreight lakes north of Campbell River can be fishing hotspots in season. Canfor's (Canadian Forest Products) logging railway near Woss Camp is one of the last remaining lines of its kind. Highway 19 skirts Nimpkish Lake and its impressive mountain backdrop. Backroaders can cut off the highway and follow backroads to Telegraph Cove (a settlement built on pilings) or journey on logging roads to Zeballos. The views of Broughton Strait are impressive on a clear day.

Access:

In Campbell River, Highway 19 turns north to cross the Campbell River near the junction with Highway 28. This trip follows a paved highway.

Description:

I always look forward to a North Island run because that means I'll be travelling the Island Highway between Campbell River and Port Hardy. The drive is scenically breathtaking as it climbs through mountain passes and near tiny communities whose economic base is linked to the forest industry. The last section of the route was punched through in the late seventies. Prior to that, the only road to northern points was a logging-road network between Gold River, Woss Camp and Beaver Cove. (See **Trip 30**.) Travellers usually took the now defunct ferry service from Kelsey Bay to Beaver Cove. My brother and I were fortunate to board one of the final sailings of this route up Johnstone Strait, where the sighting of killer whales was a highlight.

All phases of the logging industry are evident in the woodlands that Highway 19 snakes through. Stands of old growth contrast with the

The Ripple Rock trail ends on a bluff overlooking Seymour Narrows.

uniformity of replanted areas; clearcuts and slash burns reflect a more stark reminder of logging's dominance on the North Island.

We'll start out at the junction of Highway 28 and Highway 19, at Campbell River. Reset your odometer when you cut right at this corner. You'll pass the Fletcher Challenge Elk Falls mills and soon hit the left turn for Loveland Bay (km 5.3/mi 3.3), a recreation site on Campbell Lake. This road is just one access to the Sayward Forest region, described in **Trip 28**.

The Seymour Narrows lookout (km 10.8/mi 6.7) offers a viewpoint to Discovery Passage and Race Point. Over the years, more than 120 vessels had sustained damage when they struck Ripple Rock, a submerged rock outcropping right below the surface of the narrows. On April 5, 1958, high explosives were used to blow up this navigational threat, in the largest non-nuclear explosion in the world. You can take a closer look by hiking the Ripple Rock Trail. The trailhead, right on Highway 19 at km 16.7 (mi 10.4), stretches about 4 km (2.5 mi) to a bluff overlooking Seymour Narrows. Surging tides in this waterway create whirlpools and standing waves that still require respect from boaters negotiating the channel.

A tad before the Ripple Rock Trail is MacMillan Bloedel's Menzies Main, the primary access for the Sayward Forest. This region is dotted with fishing and paddling lakes — the Sayward Forest Canoe Route traverses the heart of the district — and there are countless backroads to explore. **Trip 28** offers a taste of this region, situated to the northwest of Campbell River. Watch for the Menzies Main signpost at km 14.4 (mi 9).

Near the Roberts Lake rest area, a secondary spur connects with the

Morning mist dissipates on McCreight Lake, north of Campbell River.

Island Highway, angling in to Highway 19 on the left, just over the 30- km (18.6-mi) mark. Four-wheelers should have no problem on this alternate road into the Sayward Forest; those with regular cars may find the route impassable due to deep waterholes, potholes and washed out grades.

Before you reach the Amor de Cosmos Creek bridge (km 40.5/ mi 25), you'll pass three B.C. Forest Service roads going in to wilderness campsites on a series of lakes: Stella, Pye and McCreight lakes. The condition of these backroads is directly related to the time of year and the amount of maintenance the roads have received. You can wend down to Rock Bay to look out onto East Thurlow Island. Some salt-water anglers bring cartoppers to this point and launch into the saltchuck for salmon fishing.

The Sayward junction is at km 63.7 (mi 39.6). A right here will bring you to the communities of Sayward and Kelsey Bay. Old ships form a breakwater close to the dock from which the Beaver Cove ferry used to depart. The expansive vista down Johnstone Strait makes this drive worth considering.

The Upper Adam Road crosses Highway 19 a little beyond the Keta Lake rest area. This is the cutoff for the Nisnak Meadows Trail in Schoen Lake Provincial Park. Backroaders can venture into mountainous terrain within this MacMillan Bloedel territory and loop up the Adam River Valley and down the White River watershed. The left turn for this mainline is at km 73.5 (mi 45.7). I describe a hike on the Nisnak Meadows Trail in **Trip 29**.

A signpost at km 118.3 (mi 73.5) indicates the left turn for the campsite located on the east side of Schoen Lake. Follow the signs to this provincial park campground. This road is also the cutoff for the Klaklakama Lakes on the Gold River road. (See **Trip 30**.) Over the summer months, visitors can stop at

139

the Hoomak Lake tourist booth (km 122.6/mi 76) for all the information they may require about this particular area of Vancouver Island. The rest stop has a network of woodland trails alongside pretty Hoomak Lake.

Woss Camp is home for the Canadian Forest Products' (Canfor) offices. The Woss Camp turnoff is at the 129-km (80- mi) mark of this run. You can take this turn and follow backroads along the west side of the Nimpkish River to then hook into the Gold River road near Vernon Lake. (See **Trip 30.**) It's about 65 km (40 mi) from Woss Camp to Port McNeill. The logging railway crosses Highway 19 a number of times in this stretch. This Canfor railroad extends from Vernon Camp to Beaver Cove.

Near Steele Creek (24 km/15 mi from Woss Camp) is the start of the gravel road to Zeballos. Years ago, the Zeballos area was the site of booming gold and iron mines. Some of the old workings are now points of interest. Zeballos is a stopping point for the *M.V. Uchuck III* on its run from Gold River. There are campsites near the townsite and one at Fair Harbour, further to the west of Zeballos. Kayakers often launch from here for water explorations of Kyuquot Sound. Take care on these roads as they are shared with industrial traffic.

Even if you don't venture the 41 km (25.5 mi) to Zeballos, you might want to stop at some fresh-water lakes nearer the highway cutoff. Anutz Lake, where a logging camp once stood, has 12 wilderness sites and a boat launch. Paddlers can take a connecting stream from Anutz Lake to Nimpkish Lake, the largest lake on northern Vancouver Island. Little Hustan Caves Park is close to Anutz Lake. Atluck Lake's access road is about 9 km (5.6 mi) from the highway. There is a 10 site wilderness campground at this lake. Both Atluck and Anutz lakes provide fishermen with good spring and fall trout angling.

I remember one fishing trip at Anutz Lake. We quickly set up camp and headed off to the lake. Two of us paddled my canoe to a rocky shoreline on the far side of Anutz. The third member of our party donned his chest waders to try some shoreline angling. Suddenly a yell echoed out over the waters coming from the direction of camp. As we glanced over that way, we could hear splashing and saw our friend wading back to shore. We thought he had caught a fish, so we reeled in and skimmed back to our site to investigate the commotion.

Upon landing, we noticed that our partner had somehow soaked himself and filled his waders with icy lake water. Apparently the lure of a submerged mess of beer bottles and an undetected hole in the lake bottom had combined to cause the unexpected dunking. He quickly changed his clothes and dried out near a hastily built fire.

Travellers can turn right from Highway 19 near the Zeballos Road and follow Fletcher Challenge mainlines north to Beaver Cove. This route skirts Bonanza Lake and its wilderness campsite and then passes Ida Lake, and a boat launch on the latter's shores. This 29-km (18-mi) route is a hauling road in some sections, so travelling after working hours is advisable. You might want to drive to Telegraph Cove, a unique village built almost entirely on pilings. It is one of the last boardwalk settlements on the West Coast. Close by is Beaver Cove, with its bustling log-sorting grounds. It was at Beaver Cove that Kelsey Bay ferry travellers used to disembark from the North Island ferry service.

The Island Highway heads north from the Zeballos cutoff and runs through the community of Nimpkish and then along the east side of Nimpkish Lake. There are some spectacular views of Nimpkish Lake in this stretch and the jagged mountains of the Karmutzen Range dominate the lake's western shore. Nimpkish Lake is rapidly gaining a reputation as an excellent location for sailboarding; the area has strong winds. Paddlers should travel early in the morning on the Nimpkish as afternoon gusts create heavy wave action later in the day.

Just beyond the Beaver Cove Road junction, Highway 19 crosses the Nimpkish River bridge where the river drains out of Nimpkish Lake. Right before the bridge is a road on the left leading to the Cheslakees campsite alongside the river. There are 24 sites here. The Nimpkish River is tidal at this point so anyone venturing out on its waters should be careful.

It's 7 km (4.3 mi) to the Port McNeill turn from the Beaver Cove Road intersection. Turn right here for Port McNeill. This town began as a fishing community and is now a lumbering hub as well. A ferry connects Alert Bay, on Cormorant Island, with the town. Alert Bay is an Indian village noted for its Kwakiutl totem poles. The ferry service also runs to Sointula, a fishing community on Malcolm Island.

The main offices for the Regional District of Mount Waddington are located in Port McNeill. Complete North Island tourist information, including travel tips and area maps, is available here. Western Forest Products (WFP) have their office on the Port McNeill waterfront. They publish a series of logging-road maps of their North Island divisions that can be picked up during normal weekday office hours.

A little past the Port McNeill turn are the headquarters for MacMillan Bloedel. They, too, will give visitors copies of logging road guides for their North Island woodlands. The world's largest burl is a point of interest at the entrance to their office complex. West Main intersects Highway 19 nearby. This is the start of the jaunt through Mac/Blo's Port McNeill division, highlighted in **Trip 31**.

Between this point and the Port Alice Highway, you'll notice the trees are smaller and not as grand as those in the Nimpkish Valley. Several fine viewpoints looking out onto Broughton Strait make this part of the run a treat for travellers. The Port Alice Highway junction is around 20 km (12.4

mi) west of the Port McNeill turn. **Trip 32** looks at the drive to the logging town of Port Alice, on Neroutsos Inlet. Right before this intersection, you'll pass a thermal power plant near the Keough River bridge. This one-lane span has a traffic light which alternately allows traffic through. You may decide to journey to Coal Harbour, just south of Port Hardy. You can view the now disused whaling station — the last to operate on the West Coast — which shut down in 1970. The Utah Copper Mine is close by.

Highway 19 terminates in Port Hardy. The ferry for Prince Rupert begins its run north in nearby Bear Cove. Logging roads extend west of Port Hardy to Holberg, Winter Harbour and Cape Scott Provincial Park. We'll look at these areas in **Trips 34 & 35**.

Contacts:

MacMillan Bloedel (Menzies Bay Division) (604) 287-8881; MacMillan Bloedel (Kelsey Bay Division) (604) 282-3331; MacMillan Bloedel (Eve River Division) (604) 282-3353; MacMillan Bloedel (Port McNeill Division) (604) 956-4411; Canadian Forest Products Ltd. (Woss Camp) (604) 974-5551; Western Forest Products (Port McNeill) (604) 956-3391; B.C. Forest Service (Campbell River) (604) 286-3282; B.C. Forest Service (Port McNeill) (604) 956-4416; Regional District of Mount Waddington (Port McNeill) (604) 956-3301; Fletcher Challenge (Beaver Cove) (604) 928-3060; Canadan Pacific Forest Products Ltd. (Gold River) (604) 283-2221.

Maps/Guides:

Guide to Northern Vancouver Island,(Island Information); *Outdoor Recreation Map of B.C. No. 6* (Campbell River Region), (Outdoor Recreation Council of B.C.); *Recreation and Logging Road Guide to the Forestlands of Northern Vancouver Island* (east & west maps), (MacMillan Bloedel); Canadian Forest Products Ltd. brochure (Englewood Logging Division and Nimpkish Valley); *Beaver Cove Road Guide*, (Fletcher Challenge); Canadian Pacific Forest Products Ltd. Logging Road Map (Map No. 2: Nootka P.S.Y.U.); B.C. Forest Service pamphlet (Campbell River District); Topographical Maps: 92K3 *Quadra Island* (1:50,000); 92K4 *Brewster Lake* (1:50,000); 92K5 *Sayward* (1:50,000); 92L1 *Schoen Lake* (1:50,000); 92L8 *Adam River* (1:50,000); 92L2 *Woss Lake* (1:50,000); 92L7 *Nimpkish* (1:50,000); 92L10 *Alert Bay* (1:50,000); 92L11 *Port McNeill* (1:50,000) 92L *Alert Bay* (1:250,000).

Nearest Services:

Various communities along the route.

Trip 28: The Sayward Forest Lakes

In Brief:

To the northwest of Campbell River is an area known as the Sayward Forest. Criss-crossed by networks of logging roads and dotted with lakes, there's a wide variety of destinations to choose from whether you're a fisherman, camper, backroads explorer or paddler. There are many B.C. Forest Service wilderness campsites in this region. The Sayward Forest Canoe Route is an interesting excursion for canoeists and kayakers. Morton Lake Provincial Park, a serviced campsite, is popular with family campers.

Access:

Follow Highway 19 north from Campbell River to the MacMillan Bloedel Menzies Main, near Menzies Bay. (See **Trip 27**.) Head west on this mainline. You'll follow a gravel combined-use artery. Secondary roads may be rough and narrow; some may require a four-by- four.

Description:

The Sayward Forest, northwest of Campbell River, has something for anyone who enjoys the outdoors. The region is loaded with lakes, making it ideal for swimming, fishing or paddling. The B.C. Forest Service has established recreational sites on many of these fresh-water lakes.

The Sayward Forest Canoe Route, a 48.4-km (30-mi) loop of lakes, rivers and portage trails is a challenge for many paddlers. B.C. Hydro dams are interesting points of interest. The forest was once the site of a vast railway network, when rail logging was prevalent. Today, many of the old railbeds are now logging roads, providing backwoods browsers with a variety of arteries to explore. Old railway trestles still stand: mute reminders of days gone by.

The main access road to the Sayward Forest is MacMillan Bloedel's Menzies Main, cutting off from Highway 19, near Menzies Bay (14.4 km/9 mi north of the Campbell River bridge). Turn left at this junction and head west. The secondary road to Morton Lake Provincial Park is at km 16.1 (mi 10). Cut right here (look for the smallish signpost) and travel another 6.5 km (4 mi) to the park. One feature of this serviced site is the sandy beach on the relatively tiny Morton Lake. One trail, starting from the campground, winds through second-growth forest to Andrew Lake. This walk is popular with the kids. Adjacent to Morton Lake is the much larger Mohun Lake, part of the canoe route and a favourite with local fishermen.

Near the south end of Brewster Lake, you can cut right and head north along the east shore of Brewster Lake. It's possible to drive to the secondary road that goes in to Amor Lake and journey to the wilderness campsites there. The rutted road passes Blackwater Lake and then swings east to Cedar Lake (there is another B.C. Forest Service site here) to emerge back on the Island Highway near Roberts Lake.

From the south end of Brewster Lake, backroaders can explore arteries along the Salmon River. Brewster Lake has several boat launches and wilderness camping locations along its shores. There are a variety of put-in spots for the Sayward Forest Canoe Route. Paddlers wishing to complete the entire loop can travel in either a clockwise or a counter- clockwise direction. The B.C. Forest Service pamphlet on the canoe route gives detailed background and access information.

Beginning at Gosling Bay on Campbell Lake and heading in a counter-clockwise direction, the canoe route runs through Gosling Lake, Mohun Lake, Twin Lake, Amor Lake, Surprise Lake, Brewster Lake, Gray Lake, Whymper Lake and Fry Lake. Paddlers then can return to Gosling Bay by venturing along the northwest side of Campbell Lake, the largest in the circuit. As with any large body of water on the Island, Campbell Lake can become windswept very quickly. Keep an eye on the weather and stay close to shore in rougher conditions.

Some of the connecting rivers in the canoe route have rapid sections. There are four sets of rapids between Brewster and Fry Lakes. Most are negotiable by beginners; however, if you're in doubt as to your capabilities, simply play it safe and portage around the questionable chutes. Log jams must be portaged around and low water in some of the streams may necessitate lining canoes. The portage routes often follow logging roads; others are trails constructed by the B.C. Forest Service and are marked with signposts or ribbons.

Backwoods browsers may choose another access to the Sayward Forest region. On one trip, a friend and I drove north on Highway 19, cutting left near Roberts Lake onto a secondary road that eventually brought us to Amor Lake. We based at the primitive B.C. Forest Service campsite there and spent three days fishing lake waters. On our first night we had numerous strikes and could have limited out after only an hour's fishing. We returned more fish to their lake home than we kept.

It requires greater dexterity to consistently release fish successfully than it does to bring them into your boat. Noone is perfect, yet it's amazing how little some people know about letting a fish go. Some anglers keep the fish out of the water too long; some are too rough in extracting the hook and handling the fish; others forget to revive their unhooked catch in the water; some don't care.

The Amor Lake campsite is just one example of the countless B.C. Forest Service locations to choose from in the area. Their proximity to each other makes it possible to camp at a new lake every night of your trip. You can explore the region by coming in from the Strathcona Dam road on Highway 28 as well. This route crosses the dam and spillway and drops down along the west side of Campbell River in the vicinity of Fry Lake.

As you can see, the Sayward Forest Lakes are an outdoor paradise. Whether you camp, fish, hike or canoe, you're sure to find something to your liking in this backwoods neck of Vancouver Island.

Contacts:

B.C. Forest Service (Campbell River) 286-3282; MacMillan Bloedel (Menzies Bay Division) 287-8881.

Maps/Guides:

Outdoor Recreation Map of B.C. No. 6 (Campbell River Region), (Outdoor Recreation Council of B.C.); B.C. Forest Service Sayward Forest Canoe Route pamphlet; B.C. Forest Service Campbell River Forest District pamplet; *Recreation and Logging Road Guide to the Forestlands of Northern Vancouver Island*, (east map), (MacMillan Bloedel); Topographical Maps: 92K3 *Quadra Island* (1:50,000); 92K4 *Brewster Lake* (1:50,000).

Nearest Services:

Campbell River area.

Trip 29: Schoen Lake Provincial Park/ Nisnak Meadows Trail

In Brief:

Beautiful Schoen Lake is the focal point of this region dominated by the peaks of Mount Schoen and rushing streams. At the west end of Schoen Lake is a tiny provincial park used by campers and fishermen. At the east end of the lake, the Nisnak Meadows Trail winds down to lakeside from its starting point along MacMillan Bloedel's Upper Adam River logging road. This rugged trail goes through pristine meadows, mountains and lush forests. The five peaks of Mount Schoen and a waterfall are two highlights.

Access:

Schoen Lake Provincial Park:
Follow the Island Highway (No. 19) 54.6 Km (34 mi) beyond the Sayward junction to the signposted Schoen Lake turn east of Woss Camp. Follow signs to the park. The route follows an all-hours-access gravel road. It can be rough in the off-season and impassable in times of heavy snows.
Nisnak Meadows Trailhead:
Turn left onto Upper Adam Road 9.8 km (6 mi) west of the Sayward junction (near Keta Lake). Follow mainline 22 km (13.7 mi) to parking area on left of roadway. This road is a restricted-access gravel mainline, with some steep grades.

Description:

Schoen Lake Provincial Park
The soaring mountain scenery at Schoen Lake Provincial Park is not the only memory I recall whenever I think of that North Island locale. My first trip in, just after the region became a provincial park, I was on my way south from Cape Scott, and spent a night on the shores of Schoen Lake. It was not the best of days. It was cold, misty and drizzly. The fishing wasn't

much better — nothing for over an hour, and no sign of fish. My travelling partner had already decided the warmth of a fire was more to his liking.

I shifted from the old wharf jutting into the lake over to a large log that extended out into wavelets that were forming in the chilling breeze. I could hear the crackle and hiss of wet wood at our campfire — a few more casts and then I, too, would retire to our campsite. I was using a large spoon; trying various retrieves, all to no avail. I sent the lure out again (for what must have been the hundredth "last cast") only to have the overworked line tangle on the reel. My retrieve was halted while I loosened the line; maybe that momentary pause in the action was just what I needed because no sooner had I managed to free the line than it was suddenly yanked into a huge birdsnest.

This time there was no chance of unsnarling it. With a loud "snap", the line peeled off the rod and disappeared below the water. Out of the lake danced a good-sized trout, angrily shaking its head in an attempt to loosen the lure from its mouth. It surfaced more than once before diving to the depths. Only rapidly widening rings on lake waters marked its passing. After a few choice vocal phrases, I reached down for the net, only to discover I'd left both it and my tackle box on the wharf — a fine place for them had I been able to bring the fish in. Most fishermen have a similar tale to tell: about the fish that struck when they weren't ready; problems with faulty gear or lower-priced equipment.

The turn from Highway 19 to the Schoen Lake access road is about 54.6 km (34 mi) beyond the Sayward junction. (See **Trip 27.**) From here, follow the signs to the campsite, about 12 km (7.5 mi) in. This road can be rough, notably as you near the campsite. I've made it in without the benefit of a four-by-four; however, if your vehicle is low-slung, you may bottom out in places. Trailers are not recommended on this road.

There are 10 sites at the west end of Schoen Lake. It is from this campsite that paddlers and boaters will launch for the far shores of the lake where the Nisnak Meadows Trail drops down to the shore. The park is dominated by Mount Schoen, whose summit is 1800 m (5900 ft) high. A trail begins near the campground and follows the south shore of Schoen Lake and then cuts up the Schoen Creek Valley. The route crosses a log jam on the Davie River and hugs the mountainside most of the way to the creek. There can be deadfalls to climb over and muddy sections. Gumboots can be used, but this type of footwear is hazardous on wet logs. Markers and ribbons indicate the trail, yet it's still easy to lose your way, especially in the vicinity of Schoen Creek's mouth.

The limited number of campsites at the park make for a rather cozy stay, and prevents somewhat the overcrowding feeling that can occur at many of the larger provincial parks. Note that in times of high forest fire hazard, the park could be closed. Once seen, though, the rugged beauty of Schoen Lake Provincial Park is enough to bring anyone back for more.

The Nisnak Meadows Trail

A system was passing over the Island with scattered showers, heavy rains and gale force winds. The moisture was welcome relief after a period of hot, dry weather. The rainless stretch closed many logging roads due to a high forest fire risk.

At the time, some friends and I were gearing up for a few days of hiking near the Nisnak Trail network in the vicinity of Schoen Lake Provincial Park. A quick call to Mac/Blo's Kelsey Bay Division (to check on access restrictions for their Adam River mainline) revealed there were no closures to the north and expected rain would probably keep it that way for a few days.

It's easy, during extended hot spells, to expect the same scorching conditions wherever you travel on the Island. Such a false sense of security can lead to problems in a wilderness setting — especially if you're caught without proper gear. It's always best to expect the worst and pack accordingly; particularly if you're heading for the west coast or up into the mountains. Veteran outdoorsmen respect the capricious moods of the weather.

So, as each of us loaded our packs, in went full rain gear, extra woolen clothing and gloves. We weren't being totally negative, though; a good supply of suntan lotion was brought along as well. We might as well have left the suntanning paraphernalia at home as the rain was our constant companion. It did let up a bit, revealing towering mountain tops, still clad in snow, through a grey canopy of scudding clouds.

The Nisnak Meadows Trail leads from the Gerald Main logging road; through beautiful, rugged terrain in the Nisnak Creek Valley, to the east end of Schoen Lake. To arrive at the trailhead, follow Highway 19 to the Sayward junction. (See **Trip 27.**) From this intersection, it's about 9.8 km (6 mi) to Keta Lake. Here, Adam River Main cuts off the highway to begin its climb up the Adam River Valley. Around the 22-km (13.7-mi) mark is a parking clearing on the left. Ribbons on some roadside trees indicate the start of the Nisnak Trail across the road.

The first part of the trail is flagged through to the meadows. At times, we were forced to spread out to look for tree ribbons as the route became somewhat indistinct in the heavy underbrush. There are some creek crossings, too — on slippery logs spanning boisterous creeks. One of our party decided to ford the creek rather than attempt a high log crossing.

Hikers should be prepared for wet foot conditions as you near the meadows region. While the trail becomes more obvious here, it is almost impossible to avoid all the boggy areas. Tentative breaks in the clouds

Rugged mountains dominate the terrain near the Nisnak Meadows trailhead.

allowed us to catch glimpses of the cascading waterfall in the high reaches of Mount Schoen's South Peak. The meadows are a good spot to view these falls. You can reach them by traversing the meadowlands near Nisnak Lake and then following elk trails and the natural drainage route. It is more of a route than a trail to the falls.

Two small tarns are located in the meadows, connected by a tiny stream. Camping spots are few and far between in this section. One possible site is located near a grove of trees at the end of one of the meadows. Beyond the wetlands, the trail is again marked by ribbons dangling on trees and bushes. This part of the trail involves climbing over deadfall. Hikers must be constantly watching their steps to avoid impeding roots and branches. In places, the underbrush tends to grab you and throw you off balance. Lugging heavy packs over slick logs requires patience and good balance. Caulked boots are sometimes used by visitors.

In the mature forest surrounding Nisnak Lake are a few camping spots, the prime area being near a small stream. The smallish dome tents are ideal shelters for these sometimes tiny campsites. We set up camp on a bluff overlooking the lake and started a small fire immediately, to ward off the chill of the afternoon. In rainy weather, such as we encountered, an extra fly set up in camp will provide cover and an open outdoor area for cooking.

The showers persisted. Between the rains we saw fish jumping in Nisnak Lake. We had brought our fishing rods, but most of the fish activity was well beyond our casting range.

The trail continues to the end of the lake. After it crosses Nisnak Creek, it becomes more evident and veers away from the stream and begins its descent to Schoen Lake. There are two slides to cross en route; one an alder slide almost 200 m (656 ft) wide. The trail emerges on the shores of Schoen Lake in a grove of cedars. There are a number of places to camp in this region.

Some people canoe, kayak or boat 5 km (3 mi) to the northeast end of Schoen. They then hike up to Nisnak Meadows. Persons planning a foray by water should note that the waters of Schoen Lake are often quite rough.

The Nisnak Meadows Trail is not for those preferring a Sunday stroll. Hikers should prepare for heavy rains and strenuous hiking — over slippery logs; through wet and boggy sections; along a trail that at times, seems to peter out. The fragile meadows, and awe-inspiring reaches of Mount Schoen coupled with the natural beauty and stillness of the old forest, make a trip along the Nisnak Trail unforgettable.

Contacts:

Ministry of Parks (Victoria) (604) 387-5002; Public Information Officer (604) 387-4609/387-3940; MacMillan Bloedel (Kelsey Bay Division) (604) 282-3331; Canadian Forest Products Ltd. (Woss Camp) (604) 974-5551; Regional District of Mount Waddington (Port McNeill) (604) 956-3301; Hoomak Lake Travel Info Centre (Hoomak Lake-seasonal travel info).

Maps/Guides:

Canadian Forest Products Ltd. brochure (Englewood Logging Division and Nimpkish Valley); *Recreation and Logging Road Guide to the Forestlands of Northern Vancouver Island*, (east map), (MacMillan Bloedel); *Hiking Trails Vol. III*, (Outdoor Club of Victoria); Topographical Maps: 92L8 *Adam River* (1:50,000); 92L1 *Schoen Lake* (1:50,000); 92L *Alert Bay* (1:250,000).

Nearest Services:

Sayward, Kelsey Bay, Woss Camp.

Trip 30: Backroads: Gold River To Woss Camp

In Brief:

Until the Island Highway was completed in the late seventies, the route for those driving to North Island points was the road from Gold River to Woss Camp. Today, it is utilized by industrial traffic and backwoods browsers. Several lakes with primitive camping along their shores (Muchulat, Vernon, the Klaklakamas and Woss) lure fishermen and wilderness campers. The road to Tahsis is along this route. A tiny island in the Nimpkish River is now a preserve for a stand of old-growth timber.

Access:

Take the Island Highway to Campbell River. Follow Highway 28 for 87 km (54 mi) to Gold River. (See **Trip 26.**) This route goes along a gravel combined-use mainline. You may encounter heavy industrial traffic. Secondary roads may be rough.

Description:

On many of my North Island jaunts, I'll drive the Island Highway one way and take the backroads between Gold River and Woss Camp the other, thus completing a loop run. **Trip 26** describes the highway drive from Campbell River to Gold River, so let's head north from the Gold River townsite and take a look at some of the highlights along the gravel backroads that once comprised the only road link with northern points.

Where the gravel begins just outside of Gold River, set your odometer to zero. About 3 km (1.9 mi) along, you'll reach the impressive bridge over the Gold River. Instead of crossing this span, cut right onto a spur road that goes into Antler Lake. This lake is a favourite picnic spot for area locals and the fishing here can be good. A nature trail connects Antler Lake with nearby Scout Lake.

On the west side of the Gold River bridge, you'll see a "T" junction. A left here goes into Tahsis; to the right continues on to the North Island. On the road to Tahsis, remember to watch out for industrial traffic. The route passes Upana Lake, where you might try some trout fishing. There is a fish hatchery and small campsite along the Conuma River. You'll skirt Moutcha and Head Bays at the top of Tlupana Inlet and then swing up the Sucwoa River Valley. Two more lakes (Malaspina and Perry) appear on the left.

The B.C. Forest Service maintains a wilderness campsite on the Leiner River, just before the Tahsis townsite. Tahsis is a mill town and deep- sea port. The *M.V. Uchuck III* calls here. Tahsis is the jumping off point for Nootka Island explorers, and area waters have good salmon fishing. An annual walkathon, called "The Great Walk," follows the road from Gold River to Tahsis. This event raises money for various charities and the participants must walk the 78.9 km (49 mi) distance through rugged mountains and valleys.

Now we'll return to the Gold River bridge and resume our travels to the Woss Camp area. Muchulat Lake is around the 14-km (8.7- mi) mark. There is a wilderness campsite established by Canadian Pacific Forest Products Ltd. (Gold River). On many of my up-Island tours I've stopped overnight (and sometimes longer) at this campground. The entrance is hard to see — it's a narrow, sloping road to the left of the mainline. A second, steeper spur angles down to the boat launch a little farther along. Keep your eyes peeled for either of these entrances as you approach Muchulat Lake's east end. The thirty campsites here are rarely filled up completely (except on summer weekends and holidays) and picnic tables, fire rings and a boat launch make the site a prime stop for campers and fishermen. The dock at the north end doubles as a boat mooring and float plane terminus. It's also used by anglers casting near shore.

Muchulat Lake is an excellent canoeing lake. Paddlers should be wary of afternoon winds that come up daily. It doesn't take long for a mirror-smooth lake to turn lumpy. Water conditions can be especially problematic in the lake narrows after a steady blow.

To the northwest of the campsite, the Oktwanch River feeds into the lake. Working the strike zones at this creekmouth can be productive for anglers who prefer trolling. Muchulat Main, the logging road that extends along the north side of the lake makes a wide detour inland before crossing the Oktwanch. It's not uncommon to see clouds of dust rising from the road as huge, loaded logging trucks rumble out of the woodlands heading for the Gold River mill. Travellers should be alert for any industrial traffic on the mainlines should they be journeying through on a weekday. And if it's dry and dusty, don't forget to use your headlights.

Two Muchulat Lake campsite memories remain etched in my mind:

the northern lights glittered and danced overhead during one of my stays; on another trip, the moon slowly arced across the night sky illuminating lake waters and the shadowy shapes of the mountains with a pale, tentative light.

About 42 km (26 mi) from our starting point, you'll come to the turn for Vernon Camp. This section of the drive is now within Canadian Forest Products Ltd. (Canfor) territory. Near Vernon Camp is the start of one of the last remaining private railways in Canada. Extending from Vernon Camp north to Beaver Cove, this rail line carries logs out of the Canfor woodlands to the tidewater sorting grounds. You'll see a number of railway bridges crossing the paved Island Highway should you be travelling along that route.

Approximately 50 km (31 mi) from Gold River, you'll reach a junction. To the right goes up to cut between the Klaklakama Lakes and onto Highway 19 near Croman Lake. It's 17.3 km (10.7 mi) to the highway junction. Two wilderness campsites have been provided by Canfor at these lakes. There are a limited number of camping spots at these sites and each has a natural boat launch nearby to accommodate fishermen angling for stocked cutthroat trout and Dolly Varden (char). The rocky shoreline makes swimming at these locales somewhat tentative.

A left at the Klaklakama junction runs west to a bridge over the Sebalhall Creek. Turn left, just before this span for Canfor's campsite on picturesque Vernon Lake. There is a boat launch here, 24 camping spots and the sandy beach is ideal for summer swimmers and sunbathers. The main road crosses Sebalhall Creek and turns north. Look for the signpost indicating Kiyu Creek 2.7 km (1.7 mi) along. You can park on the roadside and hike along Kiyu Creek to the Nimpkish River where an island of old-growth timber has been preserved as an ecological reserve.

Most of the trees in this reserve are around 350 years old. They include Douglas fir, Western red cedar and Western hemlock. Over a decade ago, some foresters measured trees up to 95 m (311 ft) in height on Nimpkish Island. On a recent return visit, the tallest tree could not be relocated. Was it due to an error in previous calculations? Or had the old giant fallen victim to erosion of the river and high winds?

The region surrounding the island has been clear cut over the past few years, leaving the Nimpkish Island stand as the last remnant of the old-growth forest that once dominated the Nimpkish Valley. Travellers who can remember the area from years ago lament the logging that has gone on in recent time. To some, Nimpkish Island and its ecological reserve is far too small a monument to the majestic trees of yesteryear; unfortunately, it's all that we have left.

The mainline now heads north along the west side of the Nimpkish River. Near Frost Lake, 10.7 km (6.6 mi) from Kiyu Creek, you can take

Duncan Road, a secondary spur, along the south side of the Davie River and connect up with the road that skirts the Klaklakama Lakes. Straight ahead, on what is known as Rona Road, brings you to the community of Woss Camp, headquarters of the Canfor Company. Turn right and cross the lofty Nimpkish River bridge for the townsite and the Highway 19 junction. There is a beautiful waterfall to the right as you cross the river. Kayakers often use this stretch of the Nimpkish River when water levels are right. One of the river takeout spots is just before the falls. Two of the more popular runs in the area are on the Davie and Nimpkish rivers.

About 3.5 km (2.2 mi) from Woss Camp is Canfor's Woss Lake campground, at the north end of Woss Lake. Instead of crossing the Nimpkish River bridge, bear left and follow the signs to the campsite. Woss Lake is long and narrow and knifes its way deep into the mountains. Rugged Mountain (1875 m/6150 ft) dominates the landscape west of the head of Woss Lake. Canoeists will enjoy exploring the lake's shoreline. Woss Lake is also a landing spot for float planes. A floatplane dock and boat launch are located at the 24-site campground. The sandy beachfront is great for summer swimmers and suntan enthusiasts. A spur road extends part way down the lake's east side.

Travellers can cross the Woss River bridge (near the campsite entrance) and continue along the west side of the Nimpkish River for a 24 km (15 mi) run with several steelheading pools en route. The gravel road hooks into the Zeballos Road near the latter's intersection with Highway 19. This neck of the Island is looked at in **Trip 27**. So we've reached the end of this particular jaunt, a backroads adventure through the centre of the North Island. This may no longer be the only road up to northern communities, yet it remains an exciting alternate route still travelled regularly by backwoods browsers.

Contacts:

Canadian Forest Products Ltd.(Woss Camp) (604) 974-5551; Canadian Pacific Forest Products Ltd (Gold River) (604) 283-2221; Regional District of Mount Waddington (Port McNeill) (604) 956-3301.

Maps/Guides:

Canadian Pacific Forest Products Ltd. Logging Road Map (Gold River area); Canadian Forest Products Ltd. brochure (Englewood Logging Division and Nimpkish Valley); *Hiking Trails Volume III*, (Outdoor Club of Victoria); *Whitewater Trips for Kayakers, Canoeists and Rafters on Vancouver Island, (Betty Pratt-Johnson);* Topographical Maps: *92E16 Gold River* (1:50,000); 92L1 *Schoen Lake* (1:50,000); 92L2 *Woss Lake* (1:50,000); 92L *Alert Bay* (1:250,000); 92E *Nootka Sound* (1:250,000).

Nearest Services:

Gold River; Woss Camp.

Trip 31: The Port McNeill Backroads Loop

In Brief:

Travellers who enjoy loop touring on the backroads will not want to pass up a run on the logging roads southwest of Port McNeill. Points of interest with names like the Devil's Bath, Eternal Fountain and the Vanishing River will intrigue backwoods browsers; and there's plenty to keep hikers, anglers and paddlers occupied as well.

Access:

Near MacMillan Bloedel's Port McNeill headquarters on Highway 19 turn south onto West Main. This road is a restricted-access gravel mainline. There are some rough sections on secondary roads which could require a four-by-four.

Description:

The start of a backroads loop drive begins near the headquarters of MacMillan Bloedel, just north of Port McNeill. The world's largest burl is situated at the entrance of their office facility, right off Highway 19. Discovered in the area in 1976, the burl and its host spruce were relocated to the Mac/Blo offices as a point of interest.

There are so many things to see and do in this North Island region that if your stay is limited to a couple of days, it's a good idea to plan on visiting just one or two of the scenic attractions. Hikers, for example, have their choice of the Bottomless Lake Trail, the Skidder Lakes Trail; the Trout Lake (Lac Truite) Trail or the more strenuous climb up the Merry Widow Mountain Trail. The latter is worth the effort, revealing a panoramic display of the surrounding geography.

There are a plethora of fishable lakes in this part of the Island: tiny ones like Angler and Iron lakes to the two large ones, Alice and Victoria lakes. Boat launches or gravel ramps are found at many area lakes as well as primitive camping spots. Geological features known as karst formations (limestone bedrock) are common in this region. The action of water on the limestone has created many unusual points of interest with equally unusual names: the Devil's Bath, the Eternal Fountain, the Vanishing River and the Reappearing River.

The start of this run follows West Main, directly across Highway 19 from the Mac/Blo headquarters. Just over 3 km (1.8 mi) in, cut south onto Benson Main. West Main continues on to pass O'Connor Lake (in Western Forest Products territory) before hooking into Port Hardy Main near the paved Port Alice Road.

C Main branches off Benson Main a little further along and is the road to take if you're planning to hike the Skidder Lakes Trail. Keough Lake is the first lake you'll skirt on Benson Main. Then comes a lake chain connected by Three Lakes Creek. Angler, Three Isle and Maynard lakes comprise the link with boat launches at the last two. There is a dam at the south end of Maynard.

On one trip a few years back, an employee at MacMillan Bloedel had warned me of bad road conditions near Maynard Lake. The shoulder of the road was sagging from erosion. The tenuous spot was negotiated by driving well over to the left side of the roadway. The mainlines are just as susceptible to washouts as secondary logging roads, though the former receive much better maintenance and upkeep.

A little south of Maynard Lake, R Main cuts off to the left. This is the road to take should you be journeying to the Disappearing River or the trail to the Reappearing River. Experienced spelunkers will want to explore the Minigill Caves, also reached via R Main. At the junction with J Main, turn right. This road eventually swings north to rejoin Benson Main near the Trout Lake Trail.

Should you stay on Benson Main (which skirts Iron Lake and Trout Lake) you'll reach J Main and a signpost at around the 35-km (22-mi) mark. Turn right here for the Devil's Bath and Benson Lake. Branch M 1080 provides access to the Merry Widow Mountain trailhead. At Benson Lake anglers make use of the boat launch and good spring and fall fishing. The ruins of the Old Sport Mine, now a historical site, are nearby, overgrown from years of disuse.

Keep an eye out for the signpost for the Devil's Bath. Here you'll make a sharp left onto a steep switchback which climbs up to this strange point of interest. This geological formation is suitably named. A short walk from the parking area leads visitors to a high bank overlooking a small pond, choked with fallen trees and surrounded on all sides by sheer cliffs.

About 3 km (1.8 mi) from the Devil's Bath you'll hit Alice Lake Main.

You can follow this mainline to Port Hardy Main and then north to the Port Alice Road or you might decide to cut onto Branch 41, the access road to the Eternal Fountain. This secondary road is clearly marked. The Eternal Fountain is another example of the interaction between water and limestone. Here a boisterous creek pours over a limestone ledge and then reverses its direction to flow back the way it came through a hole in the ground.

Branch 41 connects with Port Hardy Main which you can follow south to the spur road to Kathleen Lake and some wilderness campsites along its shores. The waters of Kathleen Lake are typical of the many lakes in the area, and provide good cutthroat and rainbow trout fishing for anglers. Nothing tastes better than freshly caught, pan-fried trout cooked over a fire at a wilderness campsite. Canoeists can paddle down to where the Benson River empties from the lake and travel a little ways up the river. A friend and I once spotted two black bears romping in the logging slash in this area. The north shore cliffs at Kathleen Lake harbour the remains of what appears to be a narrow-gauge rail line, possibly connected with mining efforts in the region from years gone by. What determination and engineering prowess must have been required to construct the line; on one rock face, a tunnel had been carved through the sheer rock wall.

To complete this loop run, it's just a matter of driving to the Port Alice Road and heading east to the Island Highway. Alice Lake Main becomes Port Hardy Main which runs north through a demonstration forest to the paved road. If you're returning from Kathleen, simply follow Port Hardy Main out to the highway. As you can see, to view everything in this neck of the woodlands does require at least a few days. But even if you miss out on some of the highlights on your first trip, you can always come back at a later date for another taste of the Port McNeill backroads.

Contacts:

MacMillan Bloedel (Port McNeill Division) (604) 956-4411; Regional District of Mount Waddington (Port McNeill) (604) 956-3301; B.C. Forest Service (Port McNeill) (604) 956-4416.

Maps/Guides:

MacMillan Bloedel Recreation and Logging Road Guide to the Forestlands of Northern Vancouver Island (west map); Topographical Maps: 92L11 Port McNeill (1:50,000); 92L6 Alice Lake (1:50,000); 92L Alert Bay (1:250,000).

Nearest Services:

Port McNeill, Port Alice.

Trip 32: The Port Alice Highway

In Brief:

Halfway between the North Island communities of Port McNeill and Port Hardy is the road into Port Alice. This relatively short paved highway (25.5 km/15.8 mi) winds southwest through rolling hills to Neroutsos Inlet. Several fishable lakes are en route and the picturesque Marble River campsite is an ideal base camp for area exploration.

Access:

Drive 20 km (12.4 mi) northwest of Port McNeill to the Port Alice Road, just north of the Keough River bridge. The route is a paved highway with some hills and winding sections.

Description:

North of Port McNeill, the road to Port Alice meets Highway 19. It's not far to Port Alice on this paved highway and there's a lot to see on the way. The Beaver Lake picnic and swimming area, maintained by Western Forest Products, is on the right, immediately after you turn off Highway 19. There are some floats out in the lake and a nice beach area and picnic tables along the shore. No power boats are allowed in Beaver Lake.

A little before the Marble River campsite, a gravel mainline (Port Hardy Main) intersects the highway. You can turn left here and visit a demonstration forest and also reach several spur roads going down to the east side of Alice Lake and some boat launches. O'Connor Lake can be accessed along West Main. Turn left onto this mainline a short distance after turning onto Port Hardy Main. Western Forest Products have a boat launch here and some picnic tables.

The Port Alice Highway passes Sarah Lake and then crosses the

Snow covers a snag near the Marble River campsite.

bridge over the Marble River. On the west side of this span is the entrance to the Marble River campsite, managed by Western Forest Products (13.5 km/8.3 mi). Many people will base at this campground and day-trip to area attractions. There are 33 campsites at this location, comfort stations and a picnic area. Riverside hiking trails lead down to the Marble River rapids, one of the scenic highlights. In the summer, this campsite is a Mecca for swimmers and picnickers. Canoeists and kayakers have easy access to Alice Lake via the river, and a boat ramp accommodates anglers. Steelheading is productive at certain times of the year in the Marble River. Alice Lake is known for its cutthroat trout.

The Port Alice Highway twists through hilly terrain on its way to Neroutsos Inlet, where the Port Alice townsite and the mill are situated. The drive is a little like the road between Campbell River and Buttle Lake. The first glimpse of the inlet is near Jeune Landing where there is a public wharf and float. On one trip in, I encountered heavy fog most of the way to Port Alice. Nearing the waters of the inlet, though, the mists were dissipating as the sun began to burn through.

Port Alice was established in the early 1900s. The town was once located near the mill site. It was named (as was Alice Lake) after Alice Whalen, whose five sons began the Whalen Pulp and Paper Company. The mill has had many owners over the years. In 1936, it was operated by B.C. Pulp and Paper. Their Spry Camp on the inlet was somewhat unique — the camp and homes were situated on a massive log float. Today, the mill is run by Western Forest Products. It is one of the oldest operating kraft pulp mills on the B.C. coast.

In the mid-1960s, a new townsite was constructed north of the mill. Like Gold River, it was an "instant town." The old community was burned down and the mill workers were relocated at the new location at Rumble Beach. It's a neat and tidy village, supported by the pulp mill and related service industries and commercial establishments.

Neroutsos Inlet provides water access to the Port Alice mill for sea-going freighters. An old steamer service out of Victoria used to run along the coast to Port Alice. The *Princess Norah* and *Princess Maquinna* were two vessels employed on the route. They would ply the waters of Quatsino Sound. Neroutsos Inlet is one of the long arms of that sound and was named after C.D. Neroutsos, a former manager of B.C. Steamships.

You can drive beyond the mill and cut up a steep road that goes into Victoria Lake. Western Forest Products have established a wilderness campsite at Spruce Bay. There are 10 sites here, a boat launch and picnic tables. Access can be limited to this locale, so it's best to check with WFP beforehand.

As well as the scenic value of the area, the Port Alice region offers fishing and diving in the inlet and hunting and hiking in the nearby mountains. It's close to logging-road networks that will intrigue curious backwoods browsers. Mahatta River is now accessible via logging roads extending past the Port Alice mill. This jaunt, well worth consideration, is detailed in **Trip 33**. Even if you're not planning on staying overnight in the Port Alice area, a day trip to the region will certainly not disappoint.

Contacts:

Regional District of Mount Waddington (Port McNeill) (604) 956-3301; Western Forest Products (Port McNeill) (604) 956-3391; MacMillan Bloedel (Port McNeill) (604) 956-4411.

Maps/Guides:

Recreation and Logging Road Guide to the Forestlands of Northern Vancouver Island, (west map), (MacMillan Bloedel); Western Forest Products Visitors Guide to Northern Vancouver Island; Western Forest Products Port McNeill Map; Western Forest Products Jeune Landing/ Mahatta Map; Topographical Maps: 92L11 *Port McNeill* (1:50,000); 92L6 *Alice Lake* (1:50,000); 92L *Alert Bay* (1:250,000).

Nearest Services:

Port Alice.

Trip 33: The Mahatta River Region

In Brief:

With the punching through of a logging road between Mahatta River and Port Alice in 1985, a new neck of the woodlands on Northern Vancouver Island was opened up to backwoods browsers. The 58-km (35-mi) jaunt features panoramic views of Neroutsos Inlet and Port Alice and its mill. The road link leads into the tiny community of Mahatta River and salt-water and fresh-water fishing opportunities. Restricted-access roads wind over to the west coast where spectacular vistas of the Pacific Ocean and Quatsino Sound await travellers.

Access:

From Highway 19 north of Port McNeill, take the Port Alice Highway to Port Alice (see **Trip 32**). Drive beyond the mill and onto the Marine Drive mainline. The route is a signposted gravel mainline. There are narrow sections and some steep grades. Secondary roads can be rough. Most of the route is a combined-use road; restricted access in a few sections.

Description:

Mahatta River, west of Port Alice on Northern Vancouver Island, used to be an isolated logging community accessed only by float plane or boat. Continued logging operations there, by Western Forest Products (WFP), punched through a hauling road in late 1985. This artery is now the connecting link between the area and Port Alice. It's a 58-km (35-mi) run from the Port Alice mill to Mahatta River. The mainline features some bird's-eye views of Neroutsos Inlet and the Port Alice townsite and is the gateway to new backroads for backwoods browsers.

On one trip, a friend and I stopped in at WFP's Jeune Landing office (on Quarry Main) for an update on hauling information. The employee noted on their logging road map those areas in which there was heavy truck traffic. These would be sections of our combined-use route on which to exercise extreme caution. He also suggested many points of interest, some not shown on the guide. Right below the Jeune Landing office is the dryland sort, often a bustle of activity. We passed an hour or so watching the log sorting on the flat below us.

The run into Mahatta River starts at the Port Alice mill. Drive through Port Alice and head southeast. The mill itself is one of the oldest operating kraft pulp mills on the B.C. coast. The end of pavement will be km/mi 0. The first part of the jaunt goes along Marine Drive, an appropriate name as the road follows the east side of Neroutsos Inlet to the south end near Colonial Creek. Here you'll swing north, on the inlet's west side. Cut inland on Teeta Main which follows the creek of the same name.

Just over 20 km (12 mi) from the mill, the Mahatta road begins a steep climb via a series of switchbacks and then swerves back toward the inlet. Halfway up the grade, Branch T 520 cuts off to the right. From an elevated vantage point you see the Port Alice townsite and the ever-busy mill to the south: the lifeblood of the logging town. The mainline rounds a curve and rises again, passing places where rock has been blasted out of a mountainside to allow for the road's construction. Eventually, you'll reach an area of slash burn. Then the road levels out, near the marker for the McKay Summit, over 720 m (2350 ft) above sea level. This high point is part of the McKay Ridge, a lofty plateau on Mount Pickering.

The relatively flat going is short-lived, though, as the road dives down into the Klootchlimmis River Valley. As you first begin this descent, you might wonder if you'll make it all the way to the bottom in one piece; the road is literally carved out of the mountain. Not to worry. Regular upkeep keeps the route in good shape, and it's not uncommon to see recreational vehicles and travellers pulling boat trailers behind their cars as they head into Mahatta River.

A major junction is reached just under 42 km (26 mi) from the mill starting point. K Main goes to the right to a log dump on Quatsino Sound; I Main veers left to Mahatta River. This fork is well-marked as is most of the route in. I Main hooks into J Main, near Kewquodie Creek. It is along this stretch you'll see your first glimpse of Quatsino Sound.

J Main turns south and connects with Whonnock Main. In this area, you'll be entering territory in which active hauling is common, and access restrictions play a key part of any backwoods browsing. Off-road logging trucks do some of the hauling and although the mainlines are in good shape, they can be narrow, twisty and full of blind corners. Any exploring should be done after normal working hours; and after checking on access limitations with local logging company employees, if possible.

Around the 54-km mark (33.5 mi) is another important intersection: the road to the left is B Main, an active mainline. This becomes Buck Main in the vicinity of Side Bay, a coastal indentation in the northern reaches of Brooks Bay. B Main provides access to a spur road (B11) leading to O'Connell Lake, one of the fresh-water lakes near Mahatta River. For Mahatta River, keep right at the junction. Look for the sign marking the entrance to a small, scenic campsite on the banks of Mahatta Creek, soon after you pass B Main. From this central location, many visitors set up a base camp and day-trip to other locales.

The road widens out as you approach the Mahatta River townsite. You'll notice an airstrip on the right side of the roadway. There are docking facilities for boats and float planes near the town. Salmon fishing is popular in Quatsino Sound; however, anglers should be aware of current regulations, as some restrictions apply east of Cliffe Point. Youngsters are often seen testing the calm waters of the bay from one of the mooring docks, using surf-casting gear. Beyond the dock area, the road terminates at a log-dumping ground.

Most of the logging camp buildings in Mahatta River have been dismantled with the pullout of the main WFP workforce. These included what was known as the White Bunkhouse, renowned for its rooftop barbecues. The logging currently underway in the region is carried out by small contractors, such as Le Mare Lake Logging, O'Connor Logging and Whonnock crews.

A friend of mine, who used to work in Mahatta River, related a few stories from the days when the Mahatta camp was still isolated and the road link was not in place. The main supply vessel for the camp was the *Mahatta 4*. Nicknamed "The Silver Slug" by the workers, this boat brought in supplies, groceries, machinery, loggers and visitors. Once a load of food was lost in the saltchuck when a cable snapped as the goods were being unloaded. The bay on which Mahatta River is located is usually protected from adverse wind and sea conditions, but not always. On one occasion, it was so rough that a covered dock was blown apart by high winds; a float plane was tossed on its side by heavy waves.

Camp employees would journey into camp from Port Alice on the *Mahatta 4*; if they missed the boat, they missed their shift. One of the loggers, whose position was already in jeopardy as a result of his being late too many times in the past, again failed to board the vessel at the Port Alice dock. He solved his predicament by paddling a kayak — in the dead of night — down Neroutsos Inlet to Mahatta River in a desperate attempt to be available for the morning shift. He made it just in time.

My favorite tale from the bunkhouse involved a visiting writer from a well-known magazine who spent some time in Mahatta River researching an

An exceptional viewpoint on Restless Mainline looks out over the entrance to Quatsino Sound.

article on life in the logging camp. The loggers exaggerated things a little with a series of tall tales that subsequently were published. Stories of excellent working conditions, exorbitant salaries; even yarns about drinking whiskey from caulked boots were taken at face value by the writer. After the story appeared in print, the logging company personnel office was deluged with job applications from people as far away as Alberta and northwest parts of the United States: individuals who hoped to reap the benefits that being a lumberjack in the wilds of British Columbia would provide.

Restless Mainline is about halfway between the Mahatta Creek campsite and the airstrip. This active road leads out to the west coast where visitors can view the open Pacific Ocean and Quatsino Sound from high along the cliffs near Harvey Cove. The steep slopes of Mount Bury and the Gillam Islands are an impressive sight on a haze-free day. B Main can be followed down to Buck Main or Klaskino Main for more viewpoints of the seascapes of Side Bay and Klaskino Inlet. Both Restless Main, Buck and Klaskino Main may be closed to the public due to active logging, so be sure to check with the WFP offices prior to venturing on these roads.

You can take B Main to the access road that runs along the east side of O'Connell Lake (second left from the B Main cutoff) and drive 5.6 km (3.5 mi) to an old road going into a wooden bridge crossing a narrow neck of

O'Connell's south end. You can't drive across the span anymore — large rocks and a deep ditch block the route. As mentioned previously, B11 can be followed from B Main to the west side of O'Connell and down to the old bridge. There is a small boat launch and wooden dock here near the picnic area complete with tables and comfort stations. You might be inclined to explore some of the backroads south of O'Connell Lake, along the Mahatta Creek Valley. Some of the roads are quite rough; others deteriorate rapidly or are overgrown. It certainly helps to have a four-by-four on some of these roads.

Whether you're looking for great scenery, fresh water fishing or saltchuck angling; or perhaps somewhere new to explore, the trip to Mahatta River just might fit your plans.

Contacts:

Western Forest Products (Port McNeill) (604) 956-3391; Western Forest Products (Jeune Landing) (604) 284-3395; B.C. Forest Service (Port McNeill) (604) 956-4416; Regional District of Mount Waddington (Port McNeill) (604) 956-3301.

Maps/Guides:

Western Forest Products Logging Road Map (Jeune Landing/ Mahatta River); *Recreation and Logging Road Guide to the Forestlands of Northern Vancouver Island*, (west map), (MacMillan Bloedel); Topographical Maps: 92L5 *Mahatta River* (1:50,000); 92L6 *Alice Lake* (1:50,000); 92L *Alert Bay* (1:250,000).

Nearest Services:

Port Alice.

Trip 34: Port Hardy To Holberg And Beyond

In Brief:

Five hundred and fifty-seven kilometres (346 miles) from Victoria, the Island Highway terminates in Port Hardy. But that's not the end of the line. You can continue on to the logging community of Holberg and the boundaries of Cape Scott Provincial Park on logging roads. There are some B.C. Forest Service campsites en route, fishing lakes and some notable historic points of interest worth a visit. The fishing community of Winter Harbour features a tiny yet popular campsite and many logging branch roads can be explored by backroaders.

Access:

Drive to Port Hardy and turn onto the Holberg Road, just south of town. The route is a combined-use gravel mainline with some hills. Secondary and branch roads may be restricted.

Description:

The Holberg Road begins a little to the east of the downtown core of Port Hardy. Watch for the signpost along Highway 19. We'll mark this turn as km/mi 0 of this backroads run. The road winds in past the Port Hardy municipal dump to a B.C. Forest Service Road (km 7/mi 4.3) that goes into Georgie Lake. There are a number of primitive campsites along the eastern shore of this lake. If you want to fish the area, it's an idea to have a boat or canoe along. The better fishing spots are not near the campsites; locals tend to frequent the western end or the waters of the bay on the north side of the lake.

The Holberg Road follows the Tsulquate River Valley and reaches Kains Lake at the 13.5-km (8.4-mi) mark. Here you can launch a cartopper at the gravel boat launch. Anglers may find good fishing, right from the shore, using bait and bobber or spinning lures. A tiny trail parallels the shoreline

This graphic signpost is found north of Nahwitti Lake.

leading to other casting spots.

The next part of the route runs through a logged-off area to the north of the Nahwitti River. The road swings south to cross a small bridge over the stream. In the fall, you might catch a glimpse of a motionless eagle perched in a streamside tree. They frequent this region when the salmon are running.

Nahwitti Lake is at the 25-km (15.5-mi) mark. Here there is another gravel boat launch and two B.C. Forest Service facilities: the Sandfly picnic site and the Sandfly wilderness campsite, spaced fairly close together. The campsite has toilets, fire pits, a lake trail and a limited number of camping spots beneath a stand of tall trees. The overhead canopy of these trees is so thick that even after the rains have stopped, you still might think it's raining. So moisture-laden are the branches that long after the sun has revealed itself, the heavy drops from the foliage continue to drum down on a tent fly or a camper roof. Nahwitti Lake is said to hold large trout, and on a future North Island tour, an angling buddy and I hope to spend a few days at the Forest Service location for some fishing and canoeing.

Beyond Nahwitti Lake, the road climbs a long grade. At the top of the hill is a weathered signpost that reads "Be Prepared For The Unexpected." The sign is nailed onto a large log sitting atop a crushed late model car — a reminder to visitors that the logging road is used by heavy equipment, industrial vehicles and loaded logging trucks. Caution should be exercised by those driving through, especially during weekday work hours of the loggers (usually 6 a.m. to 6 p.m.). You can check on current hauling at the Western Forest Products office in either Port McNeill or Holberg during office hours. Ask for their road guides at the same time.

The Holberg Road has been improved over the years: corners have been straightened and the general condition of the roadbed is not as hard on tires as it once was. You wouldn't be able to convince a friend of mine of that, though. On a recent trip he drove us to the Cape Scott Park trailhead in his import car. After a week in the wilderness, he seemed to be in quite a rush to return to civilization and drove the Holberg/Port Hardy stretch at a fast clip. Our suggestions to slow down on the rougher sections went unheeded until it became obvious that the right rear tire had died. The jack and spare, of course, were buried under a mish-mash of packs, tents and hiking boots.

There are two steep hills as the road drops down to tidewater at Holberg. This small logging community at km 45.7 (mi 28.3) was initially settled by the Danes relocating from failed attempts at colonizing the Cape Scott region. The road intersects San Josef Main at km 50 (mi 31). We'll turn right here, onto San Josef Main, to continue to the Cape Scott trailheads. The famous Elephant Crossing signpost is at this junction. On a railway sign are two elephants: one pink; the other red. They represent the huge logging trucks that constantly rumble down the mainline when hauling is taking place.

Approximately 2.5 km (1.5 mi) beyond the elephant sign is the left turn for Winter Harbour, a tiny fishing community on a long inlet that cuts inland from northern Quatsino Sound. The Kwaksistah campground at Winter Harbour is utilized by salt-water anglers and those preferring to set up a base camp for area hiking. Grant Bay, accessed by water from Winter Harbour and through Browning Inlet or by a strenuous trek along a trail reached by following West Main and some logging spur roads, is a scenic gem awaiting those who make the effort to get in.

San Josef Main is intersected by a number of logging roads beyond the Winter Harbour turn. Stranby Main heads north to follow the river of the same name. SJ 100 runs up to Brink and Williams lakes. Raft Main heads south into another active logging area near the Mackjack River. Around the 58-km (36-mi) mark is Ronning Main, which deadends in a burn area to the north of Raft Cove. Branch RN 700, near the end of Ronning Main, is the spur to take for the Raft Cove trailhead. The relatively short but rugged route to the north end of this wild west coast beach requires traversing mudholes and deadfall. Flags indicate the trail which emerges on the beach. The mouth of the Mackjack River can be reached by travelling south along the shoreline. This is definitely not a Sunday hike, especially in wet weather; yet the fierce beauty of Raft Cove is definitely worth the effort.

An information marker near the Stranby Main cutoff describes an old wagon road that was to connect the Danish settlements at Cape Scott with Holberg. The road link that would ensure the settlers access to markets and provide a connection to the outside world was never completed. Government delays, the outbreak of WWI and the unforgiving nature of the area's geography combined to halt the road's construction just short of its completion.

Follow San Josef Main about 1 km (0.6 mi) west of the Ronning Main turn and take the road on the right into a small parking area along the wagon road. From here you can hike to the east to an old graveyard. The wagon road has been brushed out through a Winter Works program. By walking a short distance to the west on the old road, you'll soon come upon the homestead of Bernt Ronning, an early Cape Scott settler. The current caretakers of the property, Ron and Julia Moe, are in the process of clearing brush from the site, revealing still growing sections of the exotic gardens that were planted by Mr. Ronning. Among the many specimens there are rhododendrons and two magnificient monkey puzzle trees. Unlike some of the dwellings from the Danish settlement at Cape Scott, the Ronning house is still standing, although it is unsafe to go inside the old structure. A bucket, propped on the roof near the chimney, was a safeguard against chimney fires.

At the 64-km (40-mi) mark of our run is the WFP San Josef campsite, on the boundary of Cape Scott Park. And that's about as far as you can drive on the logging roads from Port Hardy to Holberg and beyond. But if you've come this far, you're no doubt planning to continue further on foot, hiking one of the many trails in and around the Cape Scott region.

Contacts:

Western Forest Products (Port McNeill) (604) 956-3391; Western Forest Products (Holberg) (604) 288-3362; Regional District of Mount Waddington (Port McNeill) (604) 956-3301; B.C. Forest Service (Port McNeill) (604) 956-4416.

Maps/Guides:

Hiking Trails Vol. III, (Outdoor Club of Victoria); *Visitors Guide to Northern Vancouver Island*, (WFP); Western Forest Products Logging Road Maps (Holberg/Winter Harbour); (Coal Harbour/Rupert Inlet); Topographical Maps: 92L12 *Quatsino* (1:50,000); 102 I/9 *San Josef* (1:50,000); 92L *Alert Bay* (1:250,000).

Nearest Services:

Holberg, Port Hardy.

Trip 35: Cape Scott Provincial Park

In Brief:

Cape Scott Provincial Park is a hiker's paradise. Wilderness beaches and beautiful seascapes are the park's big feature, but visitors should be prepared for some lengthy trekking along usually muddy trails. Many people base camp at the Western Forest Products (WFP) campsite on the San Josef River and day-trip to places like Eric Lake and San Josef Bay, the latter about 45 minutes from one trailhead. More adventurous outdoorsmen will undertake the hike to the northern tip of Vancouver Island via Nels Bight.

Access:

From Port Hardy drive on the Holberg Road to the southern boundary of Cape Scott Park where the road terminates. The road in is a combined-use logging mainline. (See **Trip 34.**)

Description:

San Josef Bay:

Tell any of your friends that you're planning a trip to Cape Scott Provincial Park, on the northern tip of Vancouver Island, and they'll probably think you're embarking on the arduous trek into Nels Bight and the Cape Scott lighthouse. There is a trail that is shorter and terminates at a more accessible west coast beach on San Josef Bay.

The San Josef Bay trailhead is just west from the start of the main Cape Scott trail; at the end of a marked logging spur road. A parking area and signpost indicate the spot. Improvements to the trail in the way of boardwalks and log bridges have cut hiking time down from 2 hours to around 45 minutes. As everyone hikes at his or her own pace, individual times will vary. Trail maintenance within Cape Scott Provincial Park serves several purposes; it makes it easier for visitors to explore the region; it cuts down on the destruction of fragile plant life and soil structure in the boggy areas; and it

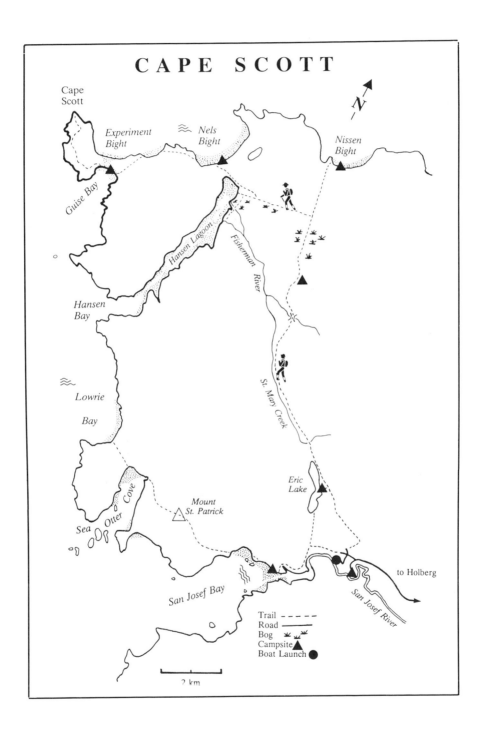

CAPE SCOTT

Cape
Scott

*Experiment
Bight*

≋ *Nels
Bight*

*Nissen
Bight*

Guise Bay

Hansen Lagoon

Fisherman River

*Hansen
Bay*

≋
Lowrie

Bay

St. Mary Creek

Sea   Otter Cove

*Mount
St. Patrick*

*Eric
Lake*

to Holberg

San Josef Bay

San Josef River

Trail - - - - -
Road
Bog
Campsite ▲
Boat Launch ●

2 km

An aging veteran of the forest lies half-buried on the windswept strands of San Josef Bay.

lessens trail deterioration.

On one trip into San Josef Bay a trio of us, laden with full packs and equipped with food and sundries for a week in the park, hiked into the bay and camped overnight on the sandy strand. The next day we backtracked to the trail winding into the south end of Eric Lake and took the somewhat rugged route that eventually linked up with the main Cape Scott trail on the east side of the lake. There were no bridges or improvements to the path across the creek draining Eric Lake. We slipped and slid our way through the rough spot to more level ground on the opposite side of the creek gulley. Had it been wetter, we would have found the boggy sections along the way almost impassable with our full loads.

On a more recent visit to San Josef Bay, a friend and I hiked in on an afternoon when the typically fickle weather sent Pacific systems, saturated with moisture, rolling in from the open sea. The beach was windswept and the bay speckled with whitecaps as foreboding grey clouds from the incoming storm swirled inland.

Many people will base at the Western Forest Products (WFP) San Josef campsite on the river of the same name. From here, day jaunts are possible to

Eric Lake or San Josef Bay. This small campground is close to the trailheads and has comfort stations, litter barrels and a wood supply. A boat launch is nearby where canoeists, kayakers or those with boats can put into the river for a run down to the bay. Tidal currents can create standing waves at the mouth, something for those contemplating a float down the river to note.

The first stretch of the San Josef Bay Trail goes through somewhat marshy land north of the river. The boardwalks here can be tricky to negotiate, especially in wet weather. For San Josef Bay, keep left at a major fork; to the right is the turn for the south end of Eric Lake. As you near the bay, the path widens out. Here you'll be walking along an old roadway dating back to the early 1900s when Danish settlers lived in the region. Some located at Sea Otter Cove; others at Lowrie Bay. At one time, cabins lined both banks of the San Josef River. The ruins of many of these dwellings are still evident, now flattened and decaying with the passage of time.

A second branch on the trail (on the left) goes down to the river. The main trail swings inland a bit to a log bridge spanning some tideland before it emerges on the sands of the beach. At low tide you can explore some of the islets on the beach or walk upriver a fair distance. At the northwest end of the beach is a water supply for those camping in the area. The trail into Sea Otter Cove and Lowrie Bay starts nearby.

This route climbs up Mount St. Patrick, the highest point in Cape Scott Park, at an elevation of 400 m (1312 ft). On maps, the distance to Sea Otter Cove does not appear to be that far, yet the informative Parks Branch brochure on the park recommends 5 hours as an approximate time in. It's 10 km (6.2 mi) to Sea Otter Cove and a further 2 km (1.2 mi) to Lowrie Bay. The climb up Mount St. Patrick takes a while and the trail is challenging and steep in places. Sections of bog may be encountered. The head of Sea Otter Cove can be inundated at high tide, so travellers venturing into these coastal areas should be up to date on tidal information. For those who make the effort, this hike is definitely worth it.

Rains and high winds are common in the Cape Scott region, even in the summer. Should you visit San Josef Bay on such a day, you'll taste a sample of raw nature much like that which the Danes endured decades ago. If the weather is good — and it does happen — the scenery will be spectacular. Either way, you won't forget a visit to the bay they call San Josef.

The Cape Scott Trail:

Cape Scott, on the northern tip of Vancouver Island, is wild, unshackled and relatively untamed. Even hardy Danish settlers failed in two attempts to colonize the area decades ago. This storm-wracked coastland is a "Class A" provincial park — and to some, the sparkling jewel in the crown of Island provincial parks. Most people who undertake the 27.4-km (17-mi) hike to the cape plan a return visit. The exquisite strands of wilderness beaches are the area's focal point and draw hikers back for that second look.

Severe storms have shaped the history of the Cape Scott region. Hikers should be equipped for torrential rains and gale-force winds. While the months of July and August are usually the driest, Pacific weather systems have a habit of appearing, even then. Rarely do Cape Scott visitors leave their raingear stashed in their packs for the duration of their trek.

The first part of the Cape Scott Trail winds through the Quatsino Rain Forest, with an average annual precipitation between 375 and 500 cm (147/196 in). This stretch can be quite muddy and using a pair of rubber boots helps keep one's feet dry. The largest body of fresh water within park boundaries is Eric Lake, about an hour and a half in from the parking lot. Many visitors opt for a day hike into this tranquil body of water. There is an A-frame cabin here (although it can be dampish) and good fishing can be found near the gravel bar at lakeside.

Trail improvements in the form of boardwalks were constructed to Eric Lake and beyond in the late 1970s. These facilitate the traversing of muddier sections and help protect fragile vegetation from the tramping of hiking boots. Some of these boardwalks have succumbed to weather and time and require careful negotiation — especially with a full pack. Aging planks have cracked at forty-five degree angles. In really dry weather (it does sometimes occur) you can skirt these broken walkways without difficulty.

Beyond the north end of Eric lake, the trail follows St. Mary's Creek. Even a short shower can create instant mudholes — quagmires at best — in the poorly-drained terrain. Numerous feeder creeks must be crossed and some use the trailbed as a route. All along this part of the trail are remains from the early settlement attempts: the old telegraph line, corduroy road remnants; even the ruins of old dilapidated cabins, now completely flattened and almost hidden in dense underbrush.

Hikers must tread carefully with intense concentration to avoid submerged roots lurking in the waterholes, or snagging branches that could cause a nasty spill. A major blowdown is evident in the St. Mary Creek Valley, with trees scattered helter skelter in the forest. On one trip into Cape Scott in early spring, a friend and I encountered a blowdown completely choking off the path. Trail maintenance crews would clear the blockade later in the season, but that wouldn't help us at the time. We were forced to slip and slide our way over the swath of fallen trees lugging our heavy packs. An extended break was called for once we had passed the problem spot and relocated the trail.

Hikers must cross the Fisherman River on a huge tree trunk which spans this waterway and has been cut square. There is a good rest stop on the far side of the river in a small clearing. This site is about three hours hiking time in from the start of the trail. A change in vegetation will be noted as you leave the rainforest a short distance along from the Fisherman River. Lodgepole pines are more common in this region, stunted by the severe climate of the area.

The forest opens up into lowlands and boggy terrain. Some of the boardwalks in this section again require careful negotiating. At an old farmsite, known as the "Dead Farm" by some, are two Parks Branch cabins. These are used seasonally by park maintenance crews. Hikers may take refuge in these sparce shelters during bad weather. The windows are missing and may require the tacking up and jerry-rigging of plastic over the sills to barricade heavy rains. Despite their austerity, the structures are welcome refuge for those caught in a sudden front. Old farm machinery and tools lie scattered about the site — rusted, mute reminders of the faded dream of settlement. A tiny stream nearby is a water source.

Next is the infamous bog. When I first encountered this obstacle I was forced to pick my way through in a zig-zag pattern and use a staff to probe possible muckholes. It was tedious and exasperating at times; especially when I misjudged my step and ending up knee-deep in a quagmire.

That jaunt was in the fall and the rains were already steady on the North Island. Since that trip, many trail improvements have been made. Small saplings have been laid down in parallel to facilitate bog passage. Some people may feel that these improvements detract from the challenge of the hike; yet in the long run, the fragile bog vegetation is subject to less damage from hiking boots and trail deterioration is minimized, and it's a lot easier when traversing the boglands now.

If you're journeying in the off-season, gumboots will be a vital addition to your footwear. If it's dry (as the summer months tend to be), you can get away with using only hiking boots. Hiking times are listed in the Parks Branch brochure on Cape Scott Park. These are general guides. Everyone hikes at his or her own pace and progress is also directly related to the weather. Once it took us 12 hours to reach the beach, including breaks. That was in the inclement off-season.

In contrast, by travelling extra light and with the benefit of one of the driest summers in years, a friend and I once made it in with our best time ever; under four hours. You should never try to overdo your hiking. Always travel at the pace of the slowest member of your party. Hurrying can lead to accidents due to misplaced steps. Maintain your patience when the going gets tough; don't fight the trail or become frustrated at your lack of progress. Some sections of the rugged route are slow going.

A signpost has been erected at the intersection of the Cape Scott Trail and the trail to Nissen Bight. Just before this point, a short path through two old fence posts leads to a forested glade where the gravestone of William Christensen is located. The adopted son of an early Cape Scott settler, young William died at the tender age of 13, as a result of a normally minor wound — a cut foot. Unfortunately, the lack of proper medical attention, due to the isolated area of the Danish settlement, and heavy seas, prevented the launching of a small boat to carry the lad to the nearest hospital in Alert Bay, 112 km (69.5 mi) away. The tragic result was that the boy died of blood poisoning. The epitaph on the granite grave marker reads: "The sun went down while it was yet day."

At the trail junction, those heading to Nels Bight and on to Cape Scott lighthouse will cut left. This goes through the heart of the old Cape Scott settlement. Little remains except the old telegraph line. There is another bog in this area and then the trail climbs a small hill to the Spencer Farm and the former Cape Scott community hall. The Spencer Farm was one of the last vestiges of the settlers at Cape Scott. It was abandoned as late as 1956. It's worth exploring this site. There are numerous farm implements in the overgrown fields and the workshop, hidden in dense underbrush, harbours old tools.

Further on down the trail is Hansen Lagoon, a wide expanse of grasslands reclaimed from the sea by a dike handbuilt by the Danes. Their first dike was washed away by high tides soon after it was completed. Hansen Lagoon is still subject to tidal fluctuations so hikers should time their arrival to coincide with low tide. In the off-season extremely high tides inundate the lagoon.

Straight ahead, the old road goes to the dike and the lagoon. The trail to the Cape cuts to the right and skirts the north side of the wetland. The Parks Branch bridge over one of the myriad bog streams is sometimes washed away over the winter. The current span has lasted a number of years, now. If it's out, you'll have to ford the creek in knee-deep water. Don't try to cross at high tide; you may find yourself taking a sudden bath. The lagoon area is muddy in spots. Stream after stream has cut deep grooves in the ground that must be carefully crossed. The wet grasses and muddy banks make the going tricky. More than one hiker has slipped along this stretch of the trail.

There is an historic signpost adjacent to the dike, at the point where the high-tide trail enters the trees. When tides are low enough, you can wade the shallows at the head of the lagoon and pick your way across the mudflats to the old dike road. Rubber boots with high tops will help keep your feet dry.

The remains of the first dike can be seen near the mouth of Fisherman River farther down the lagoon. There is an old corduroy road that winds into the site. In two places some tidal backwater must be traversed; the first on a rickety old bridge; the second on a sloping log that becomes submerged at high tide. You can walk out along the old dike to the spot where the lagoon waters have breached the old earth and rock barrier. Despite the severe disappointment of seeing their first efforts fall to nature's cruel hand, the Danish settlers successfully diked off the top end of Hansen Lagoon, creating grazing land of timothy hay for their cattle.

The sound of pounding surf increases as you approach Nels Bight through the forest. Then through one final salal patch and you're there — on the fringe of a magnificent strand of sandy beach. Nels Bight is the largest of the wilderness beaches in Cape Scott Park, stretching a length of 2 km (1.2 mi) along the coastline. A small stream at the west end is the main water supply for hikers. Nearby is a park cabin, utilized by park staff. It is not open to the public.

The majority of first-time visitors to the park will usually set up camp at Nels Bight and day hike to the lighthouse and the Cape. There are two sets of comfort stations at the beach. Following a storm, beachcombers can scour the tidelines for Japanese fishing floats; the glass balls are becoming prized mementos of a visit. You can also scramble over the rocks at Frederiksen Point to an impassable sea chasm.

Nels Bight To The Cape Scott Lighthouse:

The 8-km (5-mi) hike from Nels Bight to the Cape Scott lighthouse and the very tip of Vancouver Island is a never forgotten trek to wild beaches and awe-inspiring seascapes. Evidence of the old Danish settlements and a World War II RCAF post adds an historic flavour to the region.

The trail to the Cape begins at the west end of Nels Bight and is marked by floats in the trees and a signpost. Hikers immediately begin a climb up a hill and soon will come upon a stretch where deep ravines plunge through the forest to the shoreline far below. By following the beach at the Nels Bight and continuing beyond the lighthouse trailhead, you can scramble along the rocks for a distance (be aware of the tides) to take in the sometimes-spectacular Cape Scott sunset.

The first beach encountered on the Cape route is Experiment Bight, smaller than Nels but equally impressive. From its sands you can see the point of land on which the Cape Scott lighthouse and foghorn are situated. Many hikers take the opportunity to cool their feet in the sea by walking barefoot along the beach. The trail over to Guise Bay starts where the sand ends and the rocks begin, indicated by floats in the bushes. You can follow a rugged cliff trail to the Sand Neck by staying along the shore.

The path to Guise Bay follows an old jeep road from World War II days. Bordered by a profusion of salal, the old board roadway can be slippery and damp. Hidden in the trees as you near Guise Bay, you can locate an overgrown trail to the buildings of part of the RCAF facility that was once in

The cabin of Bernt Ronning, a Cape Scott settler, is shadowed by two large monkey puzzle trees.

operation in that area. The remains are dark and dingy, but could provide emergency shelter in the event of foul weather.

Guise Bay is a beautiful crescent-shaped beach, similar to Nels and Experiment bights but with one major difference — it's on the Island's western coast. The narrow isthmus separating Guise Bay from Experiment Bight is a giant sand dune, bordered with thick grasslands. By climbing up to a point halfway along the banks, you can view both the east and west sides of Vancouver Island. One of the early Danish settlers, N.P. Jensen, reclaimed part of the dunes by erecting a crude wooden fence. This has since disappeared over time and the dunes have reverted back to their original state. Even the old jeep road, which ran across a section of dune, has been nearly obliterated by the constantly shifting sands. There is an information signpost at the Sand Neck giving historical background on the area. There is a water source in the Guise Bay region: a tiny creek on the east end of the beach.

At the west end of Guise Bay, the trail to the lighthouse again follows the jeep road. A side trail, about two-thirds of the way in, heads out to a pocket beach fronting Scott Channel. A steep grade makes up the final leg to the lighthouse. Near the top, a side road angles off the main route and drops down to the dock where supplies for the lighthouse are brought in. Visitors from all over the world sign the guest-book register near the lighthouse dwellings. Another signpost provides historical information. Hikers should respect the privacy of the lighthouse staff. They cannot provide fresh-water to visitors.

Reaching the foghorn and the very tip of Vancouver Island requires a walk down the boardwalk path beginning near the lightkeepers' dwellings. Try counting the number of steps in the many sets of stairs along this route — it'll surprise you. Two suspension bridges span deep, sea-carved gorges near the foghorn. At the top of one final set of stairs, the cape trail ends — or does it? In the dense salal growing around the foghorn, a short path may be negotiated to a cliffside viewpoint overlooking the jagged seascape below.

Out beyond the reef-strewn Scott Channel are the wild shores of the Scott Islands. Sea lions often cavort in the swells. Commercial fishing boats and the occasional sailboat might be seen. The Scott Islands are uninhabited and frequently fog bound. Hidden reefs and dangerous riptides with their fierce currents make the surrounding waters hazaradous to boaters. Despite their inhospitable nature, the islands are home to puffins, cormorants and murres; sea lions make the Scott chain their regional breeding grounds.

The Sandneck Coastal Route:

After what can seem far too short a time at the Cape, hikers must eventually return to their camps, whether they're based at Guise Bay or Nels Bight. You can cut down the supply road and locate the start of a coast trail that winds along to the Sand Neck and farther to Experiment Bight. This route follows game trails and headland bypasses to tiny pocket beaches and coves. Watch for tides that can sever the trail and trap travellers. Be aware of the daily tidal fluctuations. In some places, the going can be rough. Mud-slicked slopes and fallen trees may impede progress. Anyone who has travelled through coastal salal knows its reputation for overgrowing trails.

It's along the sandneck coast trail that bears are likely to be in evidence. It is on this less-travelled path that these park inhabitants tend to wander on their shoreline foraging. I recall one trip on which some friends and I were completing a loop hike to the Cape via the coast trail. The bear signs we spotted on our route were extremely recent. Needless to say, we talked a lot, louder and longer as we moved along. We never saw the bear, but no doubt he heard us and knew we were there.

Nissen Bight:

While first-time Cape Scott hikers usually limit their adventure to the lighthouse trek, second- and third-time visitors often spend time exploring other regions within the parkland. Nissen Bight and Fisherman Bay are two such destinations.

Those journeying to these beachfronts will take the right trail at the junction near the Christensen gravesite. This path goes through areas of sphagnum bog to what is known as Lard Hill. There is a clay section on the way down this grade. Take care here as it can be slippery. As you reach the beach there is a fork in the trail. A tiny path to the left runs into Fisherman Bay, a semi-protected gravel beach that is often visited by black bears.

At certain times of the year, commercial fishing boats pull into the bay at sunset to wait out the night. They are usually gone at first light. You can see the fleet out towards the horizon as the sun goes down, their mast lights a flickering beacon to shorebound watchers. On calmer nights, Nels Bight also serves as a refuge for the fishermen.

The Cape Scott region dishes up some ravaging storms. Depending on wind direction, any of the bights, coves and bays can become frenzied confusions of breakers, surging seas and shrieking winds. In the late seventies, a beach landing at Nels Bight (part of a joint U.S. and Canadian Forces military exercise) was delayed by monstrous surf pounding the shoreline. A friend and I were visiting the park when the storm scudded through. The resultant breakers were indeed massive.

To reach Nissen Bight, take the right path at the trail junction. Be watchful of slippery logs and deadfall. Nissen Bight is wilder than Nels Bight. There are fewer spots suitable for camping. The water supply and best tent locations are at the east end. As you near the prime spots, the size of the beach cusps increases. These alternating, wave-formed ridges of gravel and troughs of finer pebbles and sand can be a challenge to walk on with a heavy pack. At low tide, you can skirt the softer ground and hike on the exposed hard-packed sand.

There are no comfort stations at Nissen Bight — not yet. That will come as park improvements come to even the isolated nooks in Cape Scott Park.

A little beyond the clay patch in the Lard Hill section of the trail into Nissen Bight, an overgrown trail that once led into Shushartie can be negotiated to the remains of a derelict bridge that once spanned a lake west of Nahwitti Cone. East of the lake, the trail once extended to the south of Nahwitti Cone and over to the mouth of Laura Creek. From here it cut inland near Christensen Point and ran to Shuttleworth Bight and eventually to the mouth of the Nahwitti River. Shushartie was further east. The start of the Shushartie trail is difficult to locate. Lack of maintenance and the passage of time have allowed the lush coastal vegetation to invade what was once a major link of early Cape Scott settlements.

You can scramble along the rocks at the east end of Nissen Bight, beyond the waterhole, but take care not to be trapped by incoming tides. The Parks Branch does not recommend travel in undesignated coastal regions.

Such forays should be undertaken by experienced, well-prepared hikers only.

There are some who find a journey to Cape Scott Park and a trek along its muddy trails a once-in-a-lifetime effort. The majority of visitors that I've talked to plan to return; to explore new areas and taste once again the raw atmosphere and stark beauty of the park. You can't bring the trail home. Yet those who sample the unrefined wilderness at Cape Scott will return home to a more bustling lifestyle with more than memories, photographs and blistered feet. They'll pack out an elusive intangible — peace of mind.

Contacts:

Ministry of Parks (Victoria) (604) 387-5002; Public Information Officer (604) 387-4609/387-3940; Regional District of Mount Waddington (Port McNeill) (604) 956-3301; Western Forest Products (Port McNeill) (604) 956-3391; Western Forest Products (Holberg) (604) 228-3362; B.C. Forest Service (Port McNeill) (604) 956-4416.

Maps/Guides:

Hiking Trails Vol. III, (Outdoor Club of Victoria); Cape Scott Trail Map (Maps B.C.); Topographical Maps: 102 I/16 *Cape Scott* (1:50,000); 102 I/9 *San Josef* (1:50,000); 92L *Alert Bay* (1:250,000).

Nearest Services:

Holberg, Port Hardy.

Map Sources:

As of April 1, 1989, the Maps B.C. office in Victoria no longer distributes National Topographical maps (1:50,000 scale). Provincial maps are still available at this location. These are the smaller scale charts (1:100,000; 1:125,000; 1:250,00).

You can obtain a list of federal map distributors in B.C. from the Canada Map Office in Ottawa. (See address below.) Local government agent offices may also carry a limited stock of federal maps for the region in which they operate. Some outlets will order maps for you.

Canada Map Office
615 Booth Street
Ottawa, Ontario
K1A 0E9
(613) 998-9900
(federal maps/B.C. distributor list)

Maps B.C.
Surveys and Mapping Branch
Parliament Buildings
Victoria, B.C.
V8V 1X5
(604) 387-1441
(room 110-553 Superior Street)
(provincial maps)

Island Blueprint Co. Ltd.
905 Fort Street
Victoria, B.C.
V8V 3K3
(604) 385-9786
(provincial maps/will order federal maps)

World Wide Books and Maps
949 Granville Street
Vancouver, B.C.
V6Z 1L3
(604) 687-3320
(federal/provincial maps)

Geological Survey of Canada
Sales Information Office
6th floor-100 West Pender Street
Vancouver, B.C.
V6B 2R0
(604) 666-0271
(federal maps)

Canadian Hydrographic Service
Chart Sales and Distribution Office
Institute of Ocean Sciences
9860 West Saanich Road
P.O. Box 6000
Sidney, B.C.
V8L 4B2
(604) 656-6353
(tidebooks and marine charts)

B.C. Forest Service
Vancouver Forest Region
Regional Recreation Officer
4595 Canada Way
Burnaby, B.C.
V5G 4L9
(604) 660-7500

(The following B.C. Forest Service pamphlets for Vancouver Island areas are available: Campbell River Forest District; Sayward Forest Canoe Route; South Vancouver Island.)

Regional District of Mount Waddington
P.O. Box 729
Port McNeill, B.C.
V0N 2R0
(604) 956-3301
(A composite road map of the North Island with detailed logging roads is available for $ 5.00.)

Logging Companies:
       Most logging companies offer logging road guides to travellers. These can usually be picked up at regional offices (during normal working hours), or by mail from their head offices.

Fletcher Challenge Canada Ltd. (merger of BCFP and Crown Forest)
815 West Hastings
P.O. Box 2079
Vancouver, B.C.
V6B 5H9
(604) 668-4242

MacMillan Bloedel Ltd.
1075 West Georgia Street
Vancouver, B.C.
V6E 3R9
(604) 661-8000

Canadian Pacific Forest Products Ltd. (formerly C.I.P.)
1040 West Georgia Street
Vancouver, B.C.
V6E 3C8
(604) 640-3400

Western Forest Products Ltd.
1140 West Pender Street
Vancouver, B.C.
V6E 4G6
(604) 665-6200

Canadian Forest Products Ltd.
Englewood Division
Woss Camp, B.C.
V0N 3P0
(604) 974-5551

Other useful addresses:

Ministry of Parks
Parks and Outdoor Recreation
4000 Seymour Place
Victoria, B.C.
V8X 1W5
(604) 387-5002

Public Information Officer (604) 387-4609/387-3940
Tourism Association of Vancouver Island
302-45 Bastion Square
Victoria, B.C.
V8W 1J1
(604) 382-3551/382-1665

Cowichan Fish and Game Association
Box 445
Duncan, B.C.
V9L 3X8
(A pamphlet map of the Cowichan River Footpath is available for $2.00.)

Haig-Brown Fly Fishing Association
P.O. Box 133
Station E
1230 Government Street
Victoria, B.C.
V8W 2M6
(A fisherman's map of the Cowichan River is available for a $4.00 donation to the association.)

Capital Regional District
Regional Parks Department
490 Atkins Avenue
Victoria, B.C.
V9B 2Z8
(604) 478-3344
(Many brochures on Lower Island CRD Parks are available.)

Outdoor Recreation Council of B.C.
1200 Hornby Street
Vancouver, B.C.
V6Z 2E2
(604) 687-1600
(The following maps are of interest to Island adventurers: Map No. 6: Campbell River Region; Map No. 15: Greater Victoria-Gulf Islands-Nanaimo Region.)

Suggested Reading:

Baikie, Wallace. *Strathcona: A History of B.C.'s First Provincial Park*. Campbell River: Ptarmigan Press, 1986.

Merriman, Alec and Taffy. *Logging Road Travel: Vols. I & II*. Sidney: Saltaire Publ., 1977-79.

Obee, Bruce. *The Pacific Rim Explorer*. North Vancouver: Whitecap Books, 1986.

Outdoor Club of Victoria. *Hiking Trails Vol. III: Central and Northern Vancouver Island*. Victoria: Outdoor Club of Victoria, 1987.

Pacquet, Maggie. *The B.C. Parks Explorer*. North Vancouver: Whitecap Books, 1986.

Pattison, Ken. *Milestones on Vancouver Island*. Victoria: Milestone Publications, 1973.

Peterson, Lester R. *The Cape Scott Story*. Langley: Sunfire, 1985.

Pratt-Johnson, Betty. *Whitewater Trips for Kayakers, Canoeists and Rafters on Vancouver Island*. Vancouver: Soules Book Publishers, 1984.

Scott, R. Bruce. *Bamfield Years: Recollections*. Victoria: Sono Nis, 1986.

—————. *Barkley Sound*. Victoria: Sono Nis, 1972.

—————. *Breakers Ahead*. Victoria: Sono Nis, 1970.

—————. *People of the Southwest Coast of Vancouver Island*. Victoria: R. B. Scott, 1974.

Sierra Club of B.C. *The West Coast Trail and Nitinat Lakes*. Vancouver: Douglas & McIntyre, 1987

Sierra Club of B.C. *Victoria In a Knapsack*. Victoria: Sierra Club of B.C., 1985.

Stoltmann, Randy. *Hiking Guide to the Big Trees of Southwestern British Columbia*. Vancouver: Western Canada Wilderness Committee, 1987.

Waddell, Jane. *Hiking Trails Vol. I Victoria and Vicinity*. Victoria: Outdoor Club of Victoria, 1987.

Waddell, Jane. *Hiking Trails Vol. II: Southeastern Vancouver Island*. Victoria: Outdoor Club of Victoria, 1988.

Wells, R. E. *There's a Landing Today* Victoria: Sono Nis, 1988.

Index

About the Author

Richard K. Blier has been a regular contributor to the Victoria *Times-Colonist* Sunday supplement, *The Islander*, since 1982. His outdoor articles have also appeared in *B.C. Outdoors* magazine.

Mr. Blier is an active member of the Outdoor Writers of Canada.